Hamārā

OUR BELOVED MASTER

HIS EARLY LIFE

Sheikh Muhammad Ismail Panipati

Our Master - His Early Life
(An English rendering of an Urdu book Hamārā Āqā)

Rendered in English by: Children's Book Translation Team
of Additional Wakālat-e-Taṣnīf

First published in English in the United Kingdom in 2013

Published by:
Islam International Publications Ltd.
Islamabad, Sheephatch Lane
Tilford, Surrey GU10 2AQ, UK

Printed in the UK at:
Clays Ltd, St Ives plc

For more information please visit: www.alislam.org
ISBN: 978-1-84880-091-5

About the Cover:

The Holy Prophet Muḥammad[sa] was illiterate. Therefore, he had a ring made in order to stamp letters to foreign leaders. The Holy Prophet[sa] had the ring cast in silver. He was so filled with love and reverence for Allah that he did not want to place his name over the name of Allah. Contrary to the normal way of reading from top to bottom, he had written upwards, "Muhammad Rasūl Allah".

The original seal is on display at Topkapi Palace Museum in Istanbul, Turkey along with other relics of the Holy Prophet Muḥammad[sa].

TABLE OF CONTENTS

Foreword..*vii*

PART I: EARLY LIFE

1 A Difficult Trial..1

2 An Anxious Mother..5

3 A Divine Spring..9

4 Sacrifice of a Son..13

5 First House of Worship..17

6 A Unique Prayer..19

7 A Singular Vow..21

8 A Magnificent Dream..25

9 Interpretation of the Dream..27

10 A Nation's Admiration..29

11 Broken Straw, Eaten Up!....................33
12 The Orphan's Wet Nurse....................39
13 A Bundle of Prosperity....................43
14 O Little Brave One! Peace....................45
15 Descent of Angels....................49
16 Separation from Mother....................53
17 Grandfather's Demise....................57
18 A Sacred Boy's First Prayer....................61
19 An Innocent Child's Resolve....................63
20 The Child's First Journey....................67

PART II: ADULTHOOD

21 The Outcome of Ignorance....................71
22 The Youth's Pledge....................81
23 Ṣādiq and Amīn: The Truthful and the Trustworthy.....85
24 A Prosperous Lady....................89
25 Marriage....................91
26 The Most Loyal Wife....................95
27 Corners of A Sheet of Cloth....................101

28 A Loyal Servant and A Benevolent Master........................107
29 The Dawn of the Light Of Prophethood........................119
30 King of Idols in the House of God........................123
31 Idol Worshippers........................127
32 Savage Practices........................133
33 Sacrifice of Morals at the Altar of Ignorance........................145
34 A Terrifying Scene........................153
35 Absurd Customs........................157
36 A Light in the Darkness........................163
37 The Blessed Cave........................167
38 The Angel of Revelation........................171
39 A Steadfast and Devoted Wife........................175
40 A Wondrous Event........................179

Publishers' Note 185
Glossary 187
Study Guide and Workbook........................195

In the name of Allah, the Gracious, the Merciful,
We praise Him and invoke His blessings upon His Noble Messenger

FOREWORD

This series of books was originally published in Urdu to provide children with a basic knowledge and understanding of revered figures from our religious history. Illustrations, children's activities and glossaries have been added to enhance the learning experience for children. The goal of the series is that children develop a love and appreciation for the immense sacrifices and the profound faith of the revered personalities portrayed in these books. It is also hoped that the examples of righteousness found in these pages inspire children to cultivate a personal relationship with their Creator.

This particular book is about the ancestory, childhood and early years of the Holy Prophet of Islam, Ḥaḍrat Muḥammad[sa]. It paints a vivid historical picture of the state of the Arab people at that time. Through this book children will be introduced to the righteousness and moral purity of the Prophet of Islam[as] that was apparent from the moment of his birth.

The Children's Book Translation Team of Additional Wakālat-e-Taṣnīf has rendered the series in English. Some modifications and additions have been made to the original text for the sake of historical accuracy and style. The team is headed by Uzma Saeed Ahmad and includes: Busaina Ahmad, Nakasha Ahmad, Sarah Ammar, Ruqaiya Asad, Aamna Bhatti, Haallah Ahmad Jehlumi, Hafia Khan, Rabia Khan, Rafia Rehana Khattak, Amatulhaee Mirza, Farzana Safiullah, Alia Sajid, Noma Saeed Samee, Manahil Shahnawaz, Amina Maryem Shams, Durre Sharif, and Namoode Sahar Zartasht. The team is also grateful for the valuable suggestions made by Rashidah Nasir. May Allah the Almighty reward them abundantly in this world and the hereafter. *Āmīn.*

Munir-ud-Din Shams
Additional Wakīl-ut-Taṣnīf
August 2013

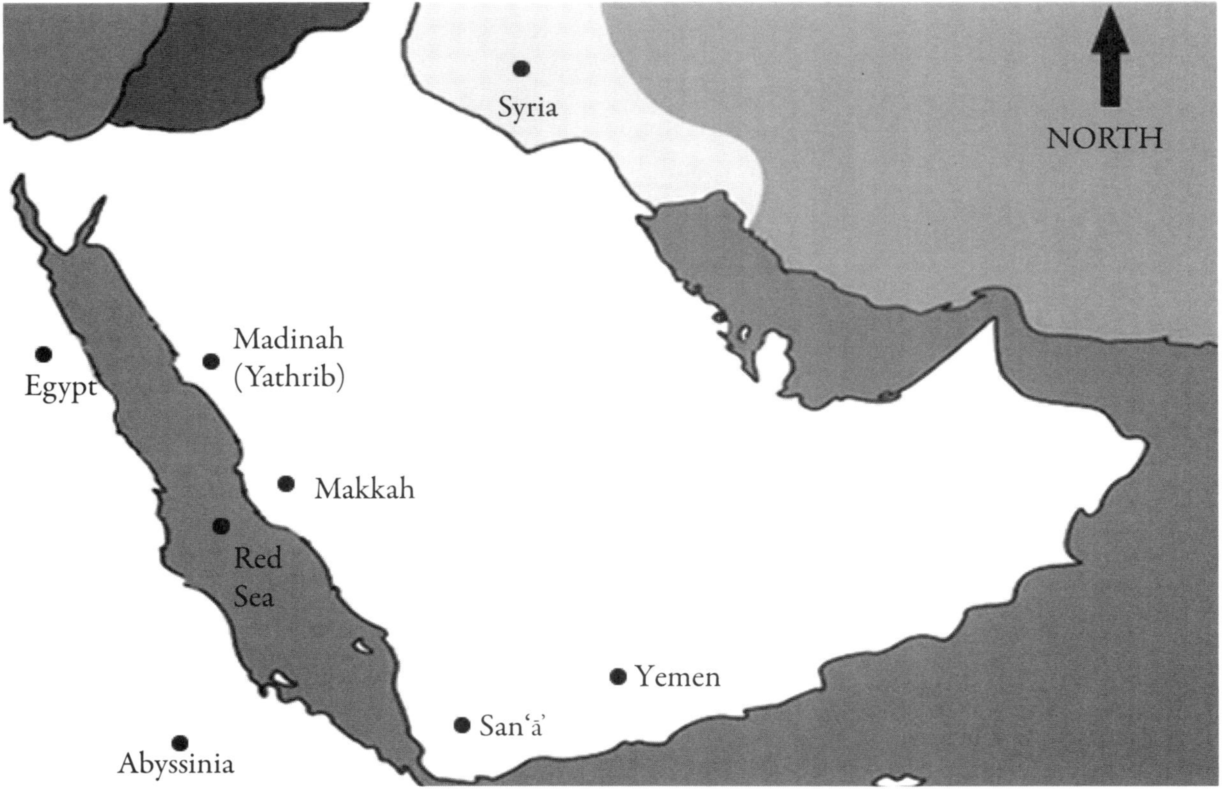

ARABIA CIRCA 700 A.D

1
A DIFFICULT TRIAL

Dear Children!

Some 4000 years ago a very unusual incident took place. In the northwestern corner of Asia, there was a land called Syria. Here lived a great messenger of Allah, whose name was Ibrāhīm[as] [Abraham]. Ḥaḍrat Ibrāhīm[as] had grown very old, but he did not have any children. For this reason he fervently prayed to God for a son.

Allah heard his prayers, and at the age of eighty-six, a beautiful baby boy was born to him. Ḥaḍrat Ibrāhīm[as] named his son Ismā'īl[as] [Ishmael] which means 'God has heard (the prayer).'

However, soon after the birth of Ḥaḍrat Ismā'īl[as],

God desired to test the child's father, Ḥaḍrat Ibrāhīm[as], by means of a difficult trial.

Allah said:

"Ibrāhīm[as]! Take the child and his mother to the bleak and barren desert of Arabia and leave them there."

The child had been born after great longing and prayer in a late age. Abandoning him in such a desolate place would surely mean his painful death.

The child's mother's name was Ḥaḍrat Hājirah[as] [Hagar], a daughter of the King of Egypt. She had been brought up in a palace surrounded by riches. To abandon her in the isolated wilderness would be to condemn her to death within days.

Although Ḥaḍrat Ibrāhīm[as] considered these dangers, his heart and devotion to God were stronger than his love for his wife and son. Taking a small leather bag of water and some dates with him, Ḥaḍrat Ibrāhīm[as] left his home to fulfil the command of God. Princess Hājirah[as] followed with her innocent child clasped to her bosom.

When this small group arrived in the desolate valley where the city of Makkah is situated today, Ḥaḍrat

Ibrāhīm[as] stopped. He placed the small leather bag of water upon the ground and handed over the bag of dates to his wife. Kissing his little child with tearful eyes, Ḥaḍrat Ibrāhīm[as] turned back the way he had come. His wife cried out and asked with anguish, "Where are you going? And with whom are you leaving us? Soon a wolf will come and devour us both!"

However, neither did Ḥaḍrat Ibrāhīm[as] look back, nor did he give a reply to her questions. Disappointed, the princess called out, "Very well, go if you must, but tell me this much. Are you leaving us here at God's command or due to some displeasure?"

Now, Ḥaḍrat Ibrāhīm[as] looked back. His eyes were overflowing with tears and his voice was lost due to his grief. Although he could not speak, he gestured in the affirmative. Upon this the princess said, "Then surely, God will protect us. Go and go without fear!" This very princess was my beloved Master's honourable ancestress, whose name was Hājirah[as].

2
AN ANXIOUS MOTHER

After the departure of her husband, the helpless princess began wondering how her life would be spent with that innocent child under the open sky and on the barren land. There was no tree visible under the shade of which she could sit for a while; neither were there any straw or sticks available with which she could provide shelter to protect her beloved one from the heat of the sun.

The princess put her precious child, who was a grandson of the King of Egypt and the son of the Prophet of Allah, on the stony ground. There was neither a palm mat nor a cloth underneath. She began to think about what would happen next.

Three or four days later, when the water in the small leather bag had finished, the little innocent child was suffering beyond measure due to thirst. His lips were parched and his tongue hung out because of the intense thirst. The mother's heart was torn to pieces at this painful sight. But where could she get water to moisten her beloved child's mouth? Thinking that her child only had a few more moments to live, the mother grew pale with fear. She looked around in desperation for water but it was nowhere to be found. She was so worried that she climbed the hill in front of her in great anxiety hoping to perhaps find a spring of water. But it was useless.

She came down and climbed another hill opposite the first one to look for water but here too, she met with failure. Then she thought that maybe the child had passed away agitated by his thirst. As soon as this thought passed through her mind, she ran down the hill and lifting the child in her lap, held him tightly.

Though the child was still alive, he had grown weak. The mother thought that she should continue to hope for the sake of survival. She thought to herself: *Let me climb the hill one more time- maybe I'll find some sign of water.*

She climbed the hill a second time and looked far and wide- but she could not find any water. Losing hope and heartbroken, the princess came down but not finding any comfort began to think about climbing the second hill to try her luck. But, there was no water!

Thus, the princess made seven circuits of the two hills, which are named Ṣafā and Marwah. She would come back each time to check up on her precious child and then climb the hill yet again in great anxiety. This sacred child, whose name was Ḥaḍrat Ismā'īl[as], was the honourable ancestor of our Beloved Master, the Holy Prophet Muḥammad[sa].

3
A DIVINE SPRING

When the mother had returned for the seventh time to check upon the well-being of her child, she saw to her amazement that at the very place where the child was striking his heels in great thirst was moist ground. There was water in that moist ground!

With feelings of utmost delight and wonder, the princess moved forward quickly and pushing away the child's foot, began to scrape the earth with her bare hands. Her joy knew no bounds when water began coming out. As she continued to scrape away, the flow of water kept increasing until it began flowing freely.

The disappointed mother's heart began to burst with joy!

Quickly, she lifted the child and gave him a drink by taking the water in the palm of her hand. The child was thus revived and he opened his eyes. The princess was overjoyed upon seeing this and immediately fell down into prostration before God who, with His divine power, had caused a spring to come out of the rocky land.

The water was still flowing and increasing in its quantity. Seeing this, the princess quickly collected stones and formed a raised boundary around the spring to save the water. The water soon reached up to the edge of the stones and a sort of reservoir basin was formed.

There was always a shortage of water in Arabia. Various tribes used to wander this way and that, carrying their camps with them. They would settle down wherever they found water for as long as there was any water; and when the water dried out, they would dismantle the camp and move on in search of another spring.

The same thing happened here. By coincidence, a tribe named Jurhum passed through and saw that a spring of water was flowing in the barren and rocky valley and a woman with a child was sitting there.

The people of Banū Jurhum desired water and said, "O

virtuous lady! How do you spend your life in this desolate valley? Who are you and where have you come from?" The princess replied, "I am a dweller of Egypt and have come here from Syria. My husband has left me here by the command of God. Allah has, with His divine power, caused a stream to come forth in this desolate place." At this, the tribes' people said, "If you allow us, we will settle down in the area around the spring. In this way we'll get water and you will not have to live in alone."

The princess was amazed at the miraculous plan of God. However, she said, "You may live here, it wouldn't harm me. But, since I am the owner of this spring, my condition is that in return for the water you shall look after the needs of food supplies for my child and me, and also that upon growing up, he shall be your chief. I want you to know that he is no ordinary boy but a grandson of the King of Egypt and the son of Ḥaḍrat Ibrāhīm[as] – the Messenger." The people of the tribe accepted both these conditions readily and gratefully and settled there.

Thus was laid the foundation of the city of Makkah, which is the religious centre of all Muslims today. The spring also exists today, though its water level has sunk below, giving it the shape of a well. This well is known as ***Zamzam.***

Certain incidents seem ordinary at first but they often have a magnificent impact later on. Take a look at this incident of Ḥaḍrat Hājirah[as] for instance - her running between the two hills was apparently something trivial but later this very incident became an unparalleled event in history. To this day, when hundreds of thousands of Muslims gather in Makkah for the observance of Hajj, in addition to performing the other tenents, they also run between the hills of Ṣafā and Marwah.

Later in history, our Holy Master[sa] climbed these historical mountains and made the first proclamation of prophethood.

4
SACRIFICE OF A SON

When Ḥaḍrat Ismā'īl[as] had grown up having been raised in the open air of the valley of Makkah, Allah willed to test his sacred father yet again. This test was even more difficult than the preceding one. God commanded Ḥaḍrat Ibrāhīm[as] in a dream, "Go and slaughter your son with a knife!"

Has such a thing ever occurred in the world? Has the heaven ever witnessed such a sight, that an aging father was ready to cut his young son's throat with his own hands? Even the thought of such an occurrence is enough to shake one to the core. Ḥaḍrat Ibrāhīm[as] was a true devotee of God. Immediately upon seeing this dream, he started on his journey taking a knife with him.

When he reached Makkah, his worthy and obedient son welcomed him with much delight and respect. Ḥaḍrat Ibrāhīm[as] took his son aside and told him, "God has commanded me to slaughter you. Consider what you think of it?"

Ḥaḍrat Ismā'īl[as] was, after all, Ḥaḍrat Ibrāhīm[as]'s son. Without any delay he replied, "My honourable father! Obey immediately whatever has been commanded. God willing, you shall find me patient and obedient."

Both father and son went into a forest. The fifteen-year-old boy lay down on the ground and the hundred-year-old father was ready with a knife to slaughter him in the way of his Lord.

The earth and all the heavens trembled at this painful sight and angels began to watch this amazing scene with great wonder. In all the histories of the world, never will one find any incident of history as amazing as this one.

How could a father's heart bear to cut the throat of his eyes' delight with his own hands? But Ḥaḍrat Ibrāhīm[as] was so overpowered by his deep love and devotion to God that he completely suppressed his normal human emotions and prepared to follow his God's command. He lifted the knife and put it to his son's throat.

Immediately the doors of heaven opened wide and God's voice was heard saying, "Ibrāhīm! Our purpose was not the sacrifice of your son, I only wanted to test your love and loyalty in this manner. You have fulfilled your dream and have passed this trial. Go! From today, I have made you the Patriarch of nations! You were ready to sacrifice your son for My pleasure. In return for this, I shall grant you such an abundance of progeny that the grains of sand and the stars in the sky may well be counted, but your progeny will be immeasurable. This is how I reward those who are obedient to Me."

Hearing this message of his God, Ḥaḍrat Ibrāhīm[as] got up from his position near his son's chest and sacrificed a lamb as a mark of gratitude.

The commandment of sacrifice on the occasion of *'Īdul-Aḍḥā* has been given to keep the memory of this incident fresh in people's minds.

5
FIRST HOUSE OF WORSHIP

After both Ḥaḍrat Ibrāhīm[as] and Ḥaḍrat Ismā'īl[as] had proven themselves to be steadfast in their devotion and obedience to God, He said to them:

"Now, both of you build a mosque for my worship in Makkah. I shall bless it so much that people will be drawn towards it from East and West."

Following God's command, both father and son built a mosque with their own hands. However, this mosque was so simple that it had neither a roof nor any door or door frame; it was a simple boundary wall. The floor within was unfinished as well.

This is the same mosque, which is known as the Ka'bah today. God has, in keeping with His promise, blessed it so much that for the past fourteen hundred years it has been the ***Qiblah*** of all Muslims. All Muslims of the world say their *ṣalāt* facing towards this very mosque and every year they arrive in the thousands to perform Hajj.

6
A UNIQUE PRAYER

As Ḥaḍrat Ibrāhīm[as] and Ḥaḍrat Ismā‘īl[as] were raising the foundations of the Ka‘bah in fulfilment of God's command, they prayed to Allah with great sincerity and utmost humility in the following words:

رَبَّنَا وَابْعَثْ فِيْهِمْ رَسُوْلًا مِّنْهُمْ يَتْلُوْا
عَلَيْهِمْ اٰيٰتِكَ وَيُعَلِّمُهُمُ الْكِتٰبَ
وَالْحِكْمَةَ وَيُزَكِّيْهِمْ ؕ اِنَّكَ اَنْتَ
الْعَزِيْزُ الْحَكِيْمُ ﴿۱۳۰﴾

Sūrah al-Baqarah, 2:130

And, our Lord, raise up among them a
Messenger from among themselves,
who may recite to them Thy Signs
and teach them the Book and Wisdom
and may purify them;
surely, Thou art the Mighty, the Wise.

This magnificent prayer was accepted in its fullest glory 2500 years later when our Beloved Master, the Holy Prophet[sa] was born in the land of Makkah from among the progeny of Ḥaḍrat Ibrāhīm[as] and Ḥaḍrat Ismā'īl[as] and the world was illumined with his light!

7
A SINGULAR VOW

The people of the Quraish were the most highly respected people in all of Arabia; and the tribe of Banū Hāshim was considered the most noble from among the Quraish. 'Abdul-Muṭṭalib bin Hāshim was the head of this tribe and a chief of Makkah. He was also respected all over Arabia for being the custodian of the Ka'bah.

'Abdul-Muṭṭalib once made such a strange and singular vow, which perhaps has never been made since the creation of the world to this day.

He said, "If I have ten sons born to me and they all reach their youth in my lifetime, then I will sacrifice one of them in the name of God."

What a Divine design it was that he had ten sons born to him and all ten of them reached their youth during his lifetime! 'Abdul-Muṭṭalib might not have thought much of it at the time when he was making that promise, but he was very restless when the time came to fulfil it. However, being a man who was courageous of heart and true to his word, he went to the Ka'bah with all of his sons to sacrifice one of them in keeping with his promise.

Upon reaching the Ka'bah, when he drew the lot, it came out in the name of his youngest son 'Abdullāh. Only seventeen years old at the time, 'Abdullāh was the most capable and virtuous of all his sons. In addition to that, he was the best looking among all the brothers. That is why 'Abdul-Muṭṭalib loved him tremendously. Besides, parents generally love the youngest child in a special way.

Therefore, at the drawing of 'Abdullāh's name, 'Abdul -Muṭṭalib was naturally very worried. Nevertheless, he wanted to fulfil his vow.

In the meantime, a number of people of the Quraish had gathered in the Ka'bah. And when they heard this, they said to

'Abdul-Muṭṭalib, "It can never be that such a capable son should thus be made to die. You should draw a lot between ten camels and 'Abdullah. If the lot is drawn in the camel's name, just slaughter the camels."

Hence, the lot was drawn a second time. It again came out in 'Abdullah's name. The people said, "Now draw the lot between twenty camels and 'Abdullah." But it still came out in 'Abdullah's name.

At the repeated insistence of his people, 'Abdul-Muṭṭalib kept on increasing the number of camels by ten each time but 'Abdullah's name was drawn every time. Finally, when the number of camels had reached one hundred, the lot was drawn in the camels' name.

'Abdul-Muṭṭalib was very happy to see this. But he drew it once more to be very sure. And this time too, it came out in the camels' name. Only then, with much joy, did he sacrifice one hundred camels in lieu of 'Abdullah.

This same 'Abdullah was the father of our Holy Prophet Muḥammad[sa].

8
A MAGNIFICENT DREAM

Among all the planets that orbit around the sun, the most beautiful and the brightest is Venus, called Zuhrah in Arabic. Named after this planet was a tribe called Banū Zuhrah.

This tribe lived in Makkah and was counted among the noble tribes of Quraish. Wahb bin 'Abdi Manāf was a prominent person belonging to this tribe.

Wahb had a daughter. She was most virtuous, cultured and of a pleasant nature. Upon growing up, she was married to the illustrious son of Banū Hāshim's 'Abdul-Muṭṭalib, the chief of Quraish, named 'Abdullāh about whom you have just read.

Three days after the marriage 'Abdullāh left for business to

Syria. On his return, having reached Madinah, he fell ill and died within a few days. When this unfortunate news reached Makkah, his wife was devastated with grief. She would constantly weep and cry in memory of her husband. It was quite common in Arabia for a widow to remarry. But this girl loved her husband so much that she decided not to marry again in her lifetime and to spend the rest of her life in the memory of her husband.

Now, most of her time was spent in mourning and lamenting her loss. She would neither eat nor drink. She wouldn't change her clothes or take care of her appearance; she would just sit still, presenting a picture of sorrow. Thus passed many months, but there was no abatement to her grief.

One night she saw in a dream that the whole world was in absolute darkness and nothing could be seen. All of a sudden an intense, bright light rose from her bosom and continued to spread and grow until it encompassed every space; and each nook and corner of the world was illumined.

The innocent lady did not understand the meaning of this dream but it did bring some solace to her grief. Do you know who this girl was? Her name was Āminah and she was the mother of our Holy Prophet[sa].

9
INTERPRETATION OF THE DREAM

Can there be any source of happiness for that unfortunate lady who was widowed within a few days after marriage? For her, the world was dark and life a prison! Finally, Allah the Almighty looked at her grief and with great compassion showed her such a blessing as had never been shown to any woman in the world and will not be shown again to another till the Day of Judgement – i.e. through an angel, she was given the glad tiding of the son who was to become the pride of all the ancients and the moderns and the spiritual master of the entire progeny of Adam.

Her happiness knew no bounds when on a Monday a son was born to her. It was no ordinary child, rather a piece of the moon, which had broken off and fallen into the lap of Āminah.

She was beside herself with joy! She took hold of him with immense love and clasped him to her bosom. She could foresee a world of happiness in the existence of this child. He was a living memory of her late husband. The boy's grandfather was informed forthwith. Seeing his grandson he was reminded of his late son and tears welled up in his eyes. Āminah gave the boy to him and said, "Before his birth, I saw in a dream – that a light emerged from within me and spread all over the world." The grandfather replied, "This child is an explanation of that dream."

This magnificent child grew up to become the spiritual master of the entire world and became the source of salvation for humankind for, because of his light, the darkness of disbelief was dispelled and the light of God's Unity illumined the whole world.

10
A NATION'S ADMIRATION

'Abdul-Muṭṭalib had grown old but never before had he seen such a handsome child. He seemed like a little angel! Carrying him in his arms, 'Abdul-Muṭṭalib went to the Ka'bah to pray for his life and prosperity.

Some respectable people of the Quraish were present in the Ka'bah at the time. They were struck with amazement at seeing the beautiful child! They congratulated their Chief and asked, "What name have you given your grandson?" 'Abdul-Muṭṭalib said, "I have named him Muḥammad[sa]." The idolaters looked at each other in bewilderment at such an unusual and unique name. It was a completely new name for them.

Finally, one man gathered some courage and asked, "O honourable chief! What is this name that you have given to your grandson? You should have given him a good name after some idol." The chief of Quraish smiled and said, "It is my greatest desire that this dear son of mine become worthy of the whole world's admiration and possesses every kind of goodness and excellence in him, and every person praises and glorifies him. For this reason I have named him Muḥammad[sa] and his mother too has had a dream which suggests that he will become a great man when he grows up." Such was the birth of our Beloved Master[sa].

No human being in the world would have ever had his desire and wish fulfilled in such an excellent manner as was the wish of 'Abdul-Muṭṭalib! Thus, you can see for yourself that to this day, no person of any status has ever been praised to the extent of the Holy Prophet[sa].

In the fourteen hundred years that have passed since him, not a single day has passed that he has not been praised in some part of the world. God on His Throne, angels in the heavens and human beings on the earth praise him on a continuous basis. It is obligatory on every Muslim to recite the ***Durūd***, in praise of his Master[sa] in the five daily prayers.

In addition to this, hundreds of scholars dedicated their entire lives to collecting and compiling his sacred words and have left exhaustive works of ***aḥadīth*** for us. Today, hundreds of thousands of people consider acting upon these sacred words a means of salvation for themselves.

Since the creation of this world, the words of no other man have been put to the pen in this manner. So many biographies of our Master[sa] have been written in every age and in every language, they are beyond count! Such a large number of biographies have not been written about any human being from the beginning of time to this day.

Thus no other guide, prophet, messenger, leader or reformer of the world has ever been praised to the extent that our Holy Prophet[sa] has been praised and will continue to be praised.

11
BROKEN STRAW, EATEN UP!

During the year in which our Master[sa] was born, seventy days prior to his birth, a frightful incident took place in Makkah, which could have resulted in the destruction of the Ka'bah and caused tremendous bloodshed. However, God saved everyone for the sake of our blessed Master[sa].

In the south-western part of Arabia is a region called Yemen, which is situated along the edge of the Red Sea. On the other side of the sea is the country of Habashah, now called Abyssinia. During that time, the King of Habashah was a Christian and the region of Yemen was under his control. The Christian governor of Yemen was named Abrahah. When he observed that hundreds of Arabs go to Makkah for Hajj every year, he was much displeased. Abrahah devised a plan to prevent them from performing Hajj by having a magnificent church constructed in the capital of San'ā'. He ordered the public to circuit the church instead of making such a long journey to Makkah. How could the people of Arabia bear a church being honoured instead of the Ka'bah? Rather than circuiting the church they sneaked up to it, littered it with filth, and ran off!

Abrahah's anger knew no bounds at this act of the Arabs. He gathered a massive force and left with sixty thousand soldiers to attack Makkah with the intention of razing the Ka'bah to ground in return for the disgrace shown to his church.

When Abrahah reached near Makkah some camels belonging to 'Abdul-Muṭṭalib were grazing in the fields outside the city. His soldiers caught them. When 'Abdul-Muṭṭalib got this news, he went to meet Abrahah.

Abrahah was thrilled when he heard that the Chief of the Quraish was coming to see him and thought that he would probably accept obedience, beg for the Ka'bah not to be destroyed and ask for forgiveness.

He greeted him with great respect and honour, seated him

beside himself and inquired after his well-being and asked the purpose of his visit. 'Abdul-Muṭṭalib said, "I have come to you because your soldiers have caught my camels. Kindly have them returned to me."

Abrahah looked at the Chief of the Quraish in amazement and said, "Of course you can take your camels back but the respect I had felt in my heart for you, having heard your name and seen you in person, has been lost. You did not have any concern for your Ka'bah, which I plan to destroy with such a large army that even if all the inhabitants of Arabia join together to fight it, not one of them will be left alive. But instead of the Ka'bah you are worried about just a few camels. The Chief of the Quraish should not have uttered such a shallow statement!" 'Abdul-Muṭṭalib laughed carelessly and said, "I am the owner of the camels and have come to get them freed. That house too has an owner. He will protect His house Himself. So why should I need to worry about it?"

Abrahah replied with a great deal of anger, " I would like to see the owner of the Ka'bah save the Ka'bah from my hand!"

'Abdul-Muṭṭalib said, "Indeed, you will see and we too shall see." Having said this, he returned. Abrahah immediately ordered his army to get ready and launched an attack on Makkah.

God's wrath descended on him at once and his entire army was destroyed. The battlefield was filled with dead bodies and there was no one left to bury the corpses. The Holy Quran has related this entire incident in a few words with amazing eloquence. Allah says in the Holy Quran:

بِسْمِ اللّٰهِ الرَّحْمٰنِ الرَّحِيْمِ ﴿١﴾
اَلَمْ تَرَ كَيْفَ فَعَلَ رَبُّكَ
بِاَصْحٰبِ الْفِيْلِ ﴿٢﴾
اَلَمْ يَجْعَلْ كَيْدَهُمْ فِيْ تَضْلِيْلٍ ﴿٣﴾
وَّاَرْسَلَ عَلَيْهِمْ طَيْرًا اَبَابِيْلَ ﴿٤﴾
تَرْمِيْهِمْ بِحِجَارَةٍ مِّنْ سِجِّيْلٍ ﴿٥﴾
فَجَعَلَهُمْ كَعَصْفٍ مَّاْكُوْلٍ ﴿٦﴾

Sūrah Al-Fīl, 105:1–6

Hast thou not seen how thy Lord dealt with the People of the Elephant?
Did He not cause their plan to miscarry?
And He sent against them swarms of birds,
Which ate their carrion, striking them
against stones of clay,
And thus made them like broken straw, eaten up.

Abrahah, Chief of the army, was punished the most. The skin of his body began to rot and shed from a number of places. He could not endure the excruciating torment and began screaming in great pain. The anger of God makes no sound when it strikes, but whomever it strikes, it does so with great force.

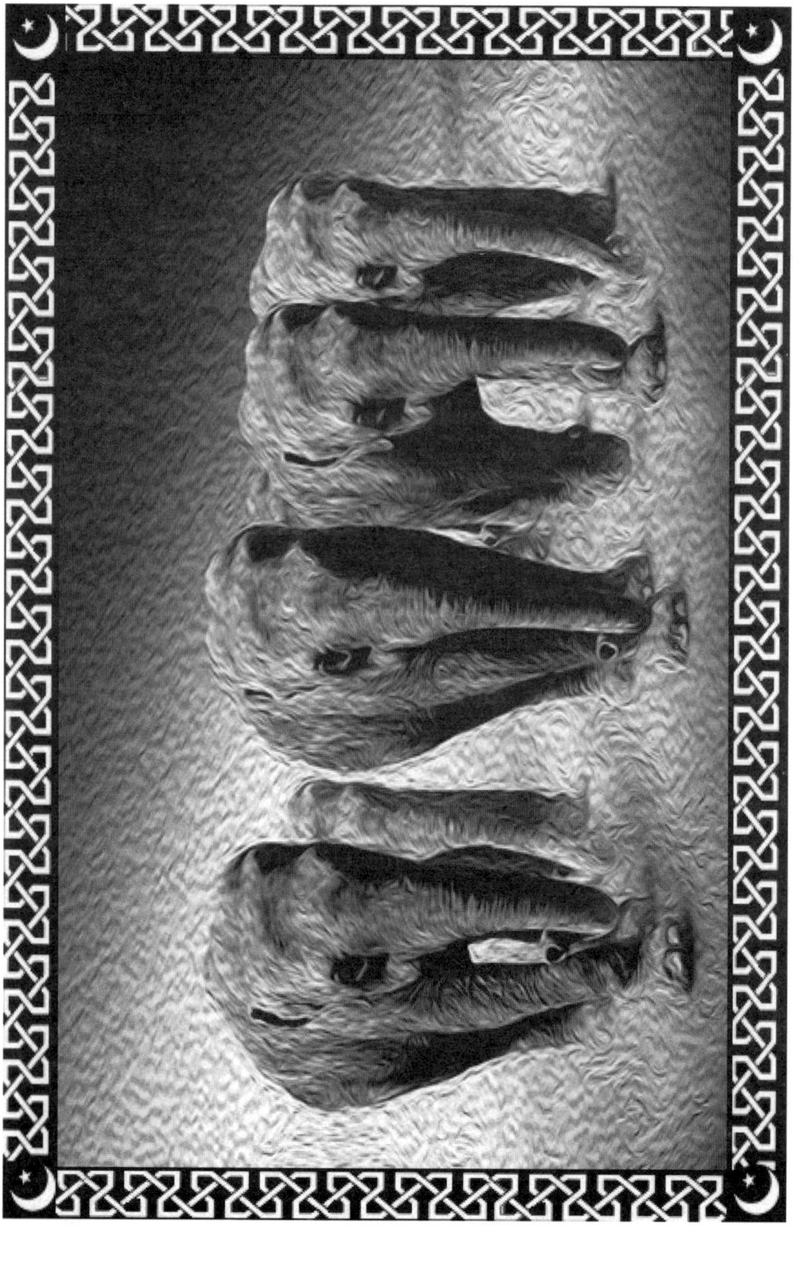

12
ORPHAN'S WET NURSE

It was a custom in Arabia that women from the countryside came to cities every six months and took home with them infants of the nobility to nurse. Thus it provided them with a source of livelihood since the parents of these children paid handsome wages for their services. And the parents benefited by the fact that their little children were raised in fresh and open air that made them fit, healthy and clever.

So, in accordance with this custom, womenfolk of the tribe of Banū Sa'd came to Makkah, at the time of the birth of the Holy Prophet[sa], seeking infants of nobility. Each woman quickly took possession of children of the rich but no one paid attention to Āminah's beloved due to his being an orphan. Orphans were generally considered bad luck in Arabia. Also, the poor mother did not have much to offer the nurse. So why would any woman offer her services to her?

Upon coming to know that some womenfolk from rural areas had come seeking infants, Āminah thought that had her child's father been alive or had she possessed much wealth, some woman would have sought her child as well. But, alas, both the factors were missing in her case, which deeply grieved the helpless widow.

Among these womenfolk was a wet nurse named Ḥalīmah. The lady was both poor and weak. Despite her best efforts, she could not procure a child for herself. She could only look at those women who had children of the rich and the wealthy with them.

Ḥalīmah was much saddened at this situation but her destiny was smiling at her and the angels were looking at her from the heavens and saying, "Ḥalīmah! You are about to get the Chief of mankind, the King of the Spiritual Empire. Just have a little patience!" When, despite her intense efforts, she couldn't get a child, she was much disappointed and asked her husband:

"If you are so willing, I can go and get Āminah's child.

Although he is an orphan and his mother has nothing to give, if I do not take any child with me, my companions will make fun of me and taunt me. Therefore, I will be better off if I work for no pay than be left unemployed."

Her husband's name was Ḥārith. He said, "This is the only thing that can be done since helplessness is heavier than a mountain. Our honour among our tribe has to be kept."

After this conversation with her husband, Ḥalīmah came to Āminah and said, "I have come to take your child. If you give him, I will take him with me."

Āminah replied, "Yes, you can take him, but how shall I pay wages for your service since neither his father is alive nor am I wealthy?"

Ḥalīmah said, "I have not come for that purpose, but have only come to take the child."

The mother said, "That is kind of you! But after all, everyone works for the other in the hope of some return."

Ḥalīmah responded, "No, I do not desire any return or wages, just the child." Thus, she took the child after much persistence.

Ḥalīmah! Little did you know that the poor and orphan

child you were taking with you would prove to be the most fortunate for you compared to all the rich and wealthy children of Makkah.

Ḥalīmah narrates: "Soon after taking Muḥammad[sa], our wants, poverty, and destitution were replaced with comfort, good fortune and prosperity. Our weak and slow-moving dromedary (female camel) became the most healthy and active of all the female camels of the tribe and our goats began producing the most milk compared to the goats of the entire family."

Though, in the beginning, Ḥalīmah had brought the child out of dire necessity without much enthusiasm, now she was beside herself with joy at her choice.

13
A BUNDLE OF PROSPERITY

The little innocent child continued to be raised in Ḥalīmah's care. And Ḥalīmah continued to be overjoyed at his sight since only due to his presence, her house had become prosperous.

Two years flew by within the wink of an eye and the time came, when generally the wet-nurses returned to Makkah to hand over the children back to their parents.

Now both the husband and wife were feeling sad since, according to the custom, neither could they keep the child nor did they want such a blessed child to leave their home. They knew very well that the child would take all the prosperity with him when he left their house.

In addition, her love for the child had grown so strong that Ḥalīmah's heart could not bear the thought of letting him go. But she was bound by the custom and brought the child back to Makkah and with utmost humility said to Āminah, "Though I have brought your child back yet I have grown to love him so much that I do not want to be separated from him. I will be most grateful if you grant me the favour of letting him stay with me for some more time. But I cannot force you, he is your child and may he be a source of blessing for you."

By coincidence, Makkah's climate was somewhat unfavourable during those days and Ḥalīmah too was most persistent. Considering both the two factors, Āminah told Ḥalimah that, "You have raised him with much love for such a long time. I do not want to cause grief to your heart. So take him with you for some more time. Besides, the climate of Makkah is unsuitable these days. I do not want the child to stay here during this period."

Ḥalīmah felt as if Āminah had bestowed a magnificent treasure on her and returned to her village most pleased.

14
O LITTLE BRAVE ONE! PEACE

The Holy Prophet[sa] was being raised in his nurse Ḥalīmah's house. When he was five years old, he began going out to graze livestock (goats) with some other children of the village. He would leave in the morning and come back with the goats in the evening. This would be the daily routine.

One day the children were grazing goats as usual in the woods when, suddenly, bandits attacked them. The children were frightened by their terrifying faces and flashing swords and ran towards the village much afraid. There was only one child who was not at all frightened, did not try to run away and stood in his place quietly. This very child was named Muḥammad[sa].

Would the bandits and looters have paid any attention to such a a small child? They gathered all the goats and were getting ready to leave when all at once the little child stepped forward and addressing the bandits, said, "The villagers have sent these goats with us to the woods; if you want to take these with you, then first go to the villagers and ask them for permission, then you can take them."

The bandits spontaneously laughed at the innocent words of the little child and without responding to him began to leave with the goats. When the child saw that the bandits had not paid any heed and were leaving with the goats, the innocent child promptly proceeded and stood in the way of the goats.

The bandits were surprised at this act of courage by the young child and said, "Move aside and let us take the goats away!"

"No, never! Kill me and take the goats with you. As long as I am alive the goats will not leave this place," said the child. The bandits looked at each other in amazement. Such a small and weak child and what bravery!

Their chief stepped forward, stroked the child lovingly and asked, "Whose child are you?"

The child replied, "'Abdul-Muṭṭalib's." There was not one

person in Arabia who was not familiar with the name of 'Abdul-Muṭṭalib. Immediately the bandit said,

"Surely, the child of the Chief of Quraish should be as brave (as you). Little brave one! I value your courage and I am letting the goats go free only because of you. The brilliance of your forehead is foretelling the greatness you shall achieve, not only among the Banū Hāshim, but also among the whole of Arabia. What is your name?"

"Muḥammad[sa]."

"Muḥammad[sa], Muḥammad[sa]. What a unique and beautiful name," said the bandit, relishing the sound of the name.

Then the bandits left saying, "O Little Brave One! Peace!"

15
DESCENT OF ANGELS

A few days after this incident, another strange event took place. According to his routine, one day little Muḥammad[sa] had gone to the woods to graze goats with the village children, when out of nowhere appeared two men with bright, attractive faces, dressed in pure white.

Without saying anything to the other children, the two men caught hold of little Muḥammad[sa]. They laid him on the ground, cut open his chest with a scalpel and taking something out of his heart, threw it aside. Next, they took his heart out, placed it in a large basin and proceeded to wash it with clean, pure water until it began to shine like a pearl. Then they put the heart back in the chest, patched it up, and left.

The village children and Ḥalīmah's son 'Abdullāh, who were watching this incident, were frightened beyond measure. Trembling with fear and out of breath, they reached the village, went straight to Ḥalīmah, and told her that a great calamity had occurred! They said, "We were grazing goats with our brother from the Quraish, Muḥammad[sa], when suddenly, two most handsome men, coming from a mountain pass, approached us. Judging from their pleasing beards, pure and chaste looks, and long, loose cloaks, we took them to be of righteous characters. But they proved to be most cruel. They quickly caught hold of our brother from the Quraish and split open his stomach with a long knife. Seeing this, we ran as fast as we could, lest they caught and slayed us as well. Who knows what happened after we left?"

Ḥalīmah was much concerned at learning this frightening news and was worried beyond measure. She was stunned and reached the field in a state of terror. There she saw little Muḥammad[sa] standing all alone.

She ran towards him and held him tightly, kissed him on the forehead and said, "My dear son! What has happened here?" The child related to her all that had taken place.

Ḥalīmah wondered why there wasn't any sign of either blood or water; neither were there any footsteps of men having been there recently, nor could she see anything that could have been taken out (from his heart) and thrown aside, nor was there any mark or wound on the child's chest. Surely the child must be under the influence of demons! She thought it would be difficult to face his mother if something bad happened to the child.

She brought the little child home and said to her husband, "I feel much frightened and cannot understand what has actually taken place. But apparently these are not good signs. It is better that the child should be taken directly to his mother. Although separation from him would be heart-breaking for us, yet what would happen if the child comes to some harm?"

The husband said, "I completely agree with you. Take him back this very day and return him to the care of his mother."

Ḥalīmah took the child with her to Makkah and returned him to his mother. When Ḥaḍrat Āminah inquired about the reason, Ḥalīmah said, "I feel as if the child has been affected by some demon."

Ḥaḍrat Āminah smiled and said, "Do not think that my child will ever be wasted. On the contrary, he will prove to be a person of high rank. I have seen unique dreams at the time of his birth."

This incident is known in history by the name of ***Shaqq-e-Ṣadr*** (splitting of the chest).

This was the first known vision of our Beloved Master[sa], which was so superior in quality that his fellow children witnessed it as well.

16
SEPARATION FROM MOTHER

Now the little innocent child began to live with his mother. It is quite unlikely for any mother to love her child as much as Ḥaḍrat Āminah loved her orphan child. But the shocking blow of her husband's demise was not such as would diminish from her heart. Whenever she glanced at the orphan child, she would grow anxious, being reminded of his father.

One day, when the remembrance of her husband became unbearable, Ḥaḍrat Āminah decided to visit his grave in Madinah so as to bring solace to her grieving heart.

Therefore she took her beloved son to Madinah and stayed with her relatives for a month.

During her stay in Madinah, it was her daily practice to visit her husband's grave and to stay there for a long time. After living in Madinah for a month, she decided to return. She did not have to wait for long. A caravan was leaving for Makkah; Ḥaḍrat Āminah joined them with her son and departed from Madinah.

When the caravan had reached a place called Abwā', Ḥaḍrat Āminah suddenly fell ill; so ill that she lost all hope of her life. When she realized that the last moments of her life had approached, she glanced towards her beloved son with intense sorrow.

The little innocent child stood there; a picture of grief. When the mother motioned him to come to her, he ran and clasped her bosom. Tears flowed from the mother's eyes.

Just imagine what a painful sight it was. The mother was leaving the world with a hundred wishes and thousands of desires in her heart. What thoughts must have passed through her heart? The grief of leaving her innocent child friendless in the bleak and barren desert caused absolute torture to her soul. Her heart was being torn apart at the thought of how the six year old would survive in the terrifying valley without her and the calamities he would have to endure. But death does not consider anyone's desires or longings; it spares neither kings nor beggars; it shows favour neither to the rich nor to the poor.

Ḥaḍrat Āminah left the world after a short while and left her beloved alone in its wilderness. How difficult was this time! The beloved child was standing next to his mother's corpse utterly bewildered. His heart was full of grief and his eyes were welled up with tears. He questioned all that was happening and began thinking about what would happen to him.

His father had left the world even before his birth; his grief stricken mother had departed the world too, leaving him an orphan at six years of age. This was the childhood of our Beloved Master[sa].

People of the caravan buried Ḥaḍrat Āminah at that very place and brought the orphan child back to Makkah to his grandfather.

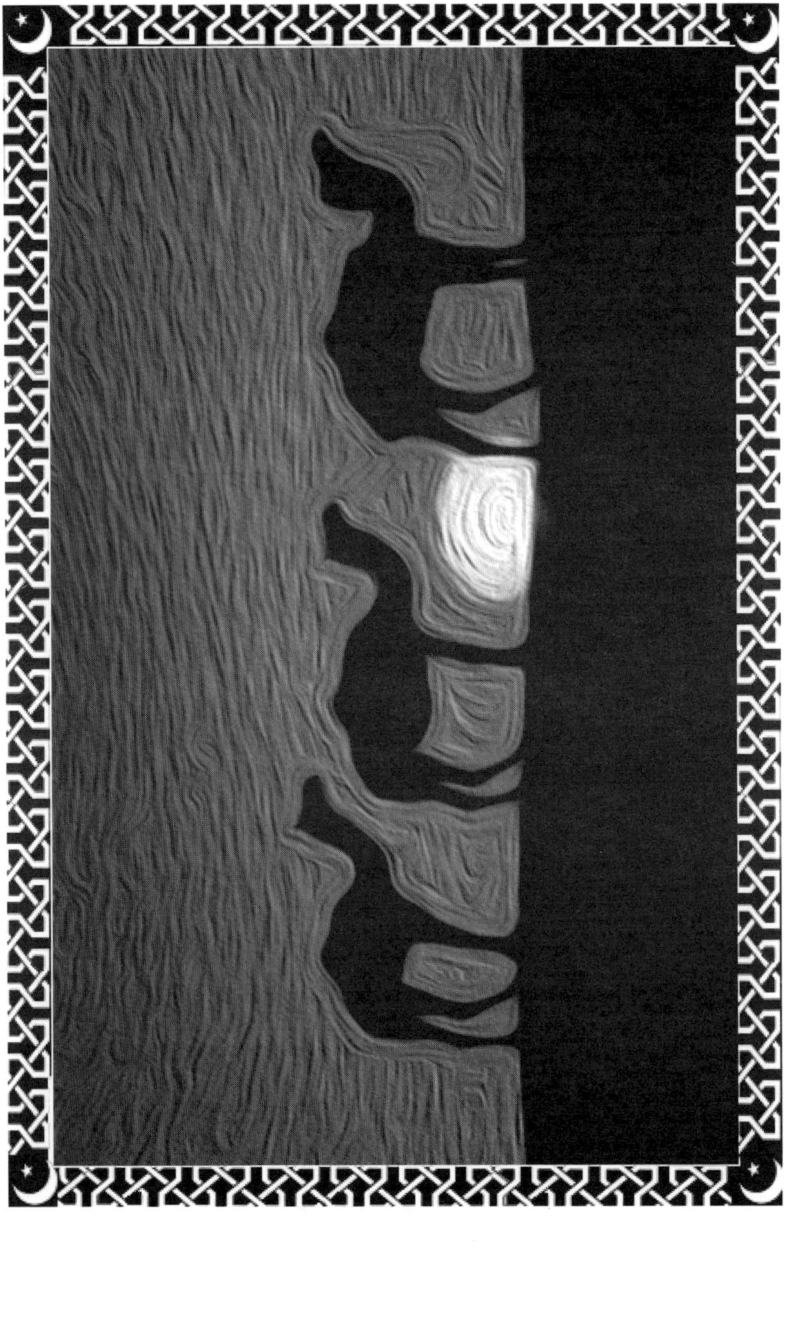

17
GRANDFATHER'S DEMISE

Although 'Abdul-Muṭṭalib had eleven or twelve sons of his own, he loved his innocent and orphan grandson the most. He would have the child eat and sleep with him and kept him by his side all the time. Since he was Chief of the Quraish and a dignified elder of the community, he usually sat inside the Ka'bah on a carpet laid specially for him and none dared to sit beside him; but his grandson would sit beside him without any inhibition. If anyone admonished him once or twice, 'Abdul-Muṭṭalib would say: "Do not stop him; he will sit beside me."

But alas! The grandson wasn't able to enjoy his grandfather's love and compassion for long. Not two years had passed when 'Abdul-Muṭṭalib was beckoned by death.

When the Chief of the Quraish realized that he was about to die, he began to ponder about the fate of the innocent child who was only eight years old; he thought of the possible losses the child may have to suffer and the pitiable state of life he may have to endure. So, he desired to appoint one of his sons as his guardian and caretaker. He asked all his sons to come to him. They all came and sat in the presence of their ailing father.

Addressing his grandson, 'Abdul-Muṭṭalib said,

> "My dear child, I have done all that was possible for me to do; given you a good upbringing and looked after your well-being. It is my greatest desire that you may become a very famous person and the whole world may praise your achievements. For this reason, I had named you Muḥammad[sa] when you were born. It was my wish to witness your exalted position in my lifetime, but alas, this happiness was not a part of my destiny. I am about to die now and shall take this desire with me to my grave. All your paternal uncles are sitting in front of you at this time. Go to the one with whom you would like to stay after I am gone and he shall be your guardian and caretaker in future."

The grandson's eyes welled up with tears at the words of his grandfather but there was nothing else that could be done. With a grieving heart, he looked at all the paternal uncles, walked over and stood next to Abū Ṭālib. Abū Ṭālib affectionately kissed his nephew and seated him on his lap. Seeing this, 'Abdul-Muṭṭalib said,

> "Abū Ṭālib! I entrust this living memory of mine to your care. Keep him with you in memory of your late brother and do not fall short in your efforts to please him. He did not see his father and did not savour the love of his mother for long. Thus, he hasn't experienced any comfort of this world and successive losses have made his heart more fragile than glass. Promise me that you will protect your orphan nephew fully and shall always treat him with utmost love and compassion and care for his needs far above that of your own sons."

The obedient son sincerely pledged to take care of his nephew to the best of his abilities. And the passage of time proved that Ḥaḍrat Abū Ṭālib delivered far above the promise that he had made to his father.

O Abū Ṭālib! Our heads bow low in reverence for you when we witness the fact that you raised our Beloved Master[sa] in such an exemplary manner.

It is worth noting here that when 'Abdul-Muṭṭalib had gathered his sons to decide who would bear the responsibility of his grandson, Abū Lahab was the one who was the most desirous of keeping his orphan nephew with him. He used to love the Holy Prophet[sa] tremendously and had even freed the bondservant who had brought him the good news of the birth of this nephew.

Strange how events can change family bonds! This very paternal uncle, so full of love and devotion, was transformed into his archenemy when the nephew gave him the glad tidings of his prophethood.

18
A SACRED BOY'S FIRST PRAYER

The orphan child began to live with his uncle, Abū Ṭālib. Abū Ṭālib cared for him even more than his own children. He would always keep him in his own company and would pay particular attention to matters of his comfort. He would never do anything against the child's will.

Abū Ṭālib was constantly amazed at his nephew's noble and chaste habits. Not only did he love the child immensely, but an impression of his greatness also became firmly rooted in Abū Ṭālib's heart.

It is mentioned in books of history that once there was a severe drought in Makkah, and not a drop of water had rained from the sky. The people of Makkah were very worried. On this occasion, Abū Ṭālib said to his nephew,

"My dear, people are much agitated without water. You are innocent of heart and pure of tongue and I observe that your existence is an admirable one. Take the people of the city with you to the jungle and pray to God for water."

The nephew answered, "Uncle, of what significance am I or my prayer? This is the job of older and nobler people while I am just a child! However, I cannot refuse to obey your order. I will pray. It is possible that although I am weak, God will accept my prayer and eliminate the drought."

Thus our little Master[sa] went to the jungle with all the noble men and the dwellers of Makkah and standing in front of the entire group raised his small hands in prayer.

It was as if the angels of the clouds had been waiting for that very moment. Immediately upon his prayer, it rained to the extent that all the suffering caused by the drought was eliminated and the desire of the Makkans was fulfilled!

For the first time ever, the Quraish realized that there was a sacred boy living amongst them.

This was the first prayer of that sacred boy.

19
AN INNOCENT CHILD'S RESOLVE

A young child, hardly nine or ten years of age, grazed goats with another boy in the mountainous fields outside of Makkah.

It was the custom of the city that various households held gatherings for story telling and poetry recitals. In these gatherings, stories about the bravery and heroism of their ancestors were narrated using ornate words and poetry.

People participated in such events with great enthusiasm. They would spend the entire evening indulging in drinking, revelry and commotion. The young child was aware of all this but had not yet participated in any such events. Yet he was just a child and had the same feelings as all children do. The people of that time were raised in such an environment that everyone was addicted to these things. The child possessed a heart filled with the feelings, longings and desires of childhood. The child asked himself why he should not experience one such gathering for a little while and see for himself what happened there.

Having thought this, he said to his companion, "My friend, I desire to see a gathering in the city today, but I have been entrusted to graze these goats. I have thought of a solution. If you promise to guard my goats, I can go to the city and experience these functions for a short while. In return for this favor, you can go to the city tomorrow and I will guard your goats."

His companion agreed to this and the young child happily left for the city to take part in the entertainments and amusements. Before he even entered the city he saw a few people assembled in a house on the border of the city.

The child inquired of someone, "What is happening here?"

Some people said, "We are getting ready for a wedding." Without giving it much thought, the child went inside the house. The floor was covered with carpets and people were sitting there, waiting for the bridegroom to arrive. The child also sat down on the floor.

As soon as he sat down, God commanded angels to blow a gentle and cold breeze such that it would put the child to sleep.

The wind started to blow in immediate compliance of the order and the child lay down on the floor and fell asleep.

When his eyes opened, it was already evening and the sun was setting behind the hills. The child stood up in confusion and anxious about his goats, left for the jungle in a great hurry. The experience had failed.

He decided that since he had fallen asleep and was not able to participate in any gathering, he would try again on another day.

Hence on another day when the weather was pleasant, the child entrusted his goats to his companion and once again left for the city. But once again, due to another such incident the little child was unable to take part in any event. After that, he developed a dislike for all such functions and he never planned on trying to attend them again.

Do you know who this young child was? He was our Beloved Master, Muḥammad Musṭafā[sa].

20
THE CHILD'S FIRST JOURNEY

The Quraish were a nation of traders. Every year their trading convoys would go to Syria, Iraq, Palestine and Egypt. They had also established trading ties on the other side of the continent from India to China. The Quraish would buy merchandise from other countries and sell the goods that they had brought from their own country.

At this time in Arabia neither individuals nor convoys were safe from bandits, robbers, and highwaymen. They robbed whoever would fall victim to them. They immediately wiped out anyone who tried to fight them. They felt neither shame in plundering nor any constraint in shedding blood. It was said about them,

"So artful were they in killing and ravaging,

They were like the fearless beasts of the jungle."

However, the Quraish had an advantage in conducting business because they were the custodians of the Ka'bah. Due to this fact the Quraish held a special place of respect among the Arabs and as a result of this reverence, the trading parties of the Quraish crossed deserts, travelled through jungles, traversed valleys and wilderness, but none dared to harm them.

They would travel in peace, laden with trading goods, to distant lands and bring back goods to Makkah. In that tumultuous age of fighting, assault and plunder, this peace was indeed a great benefit.

Abū Ṭālib was also a respected member of the Quraish tribe and often used to travel with his convoy for business with Syria.

After 'Abdul-Muṭṭalib's demise Abū Ṭālib was scheduled to go on a trading expedition to Syria, leaving behind his nephew who was only ten years old.

Abū Ṭālib loved his nephew intensely and never wanted

to be apart from him. However since the route was arduous and difficult to reach, and because he could not bear his nephew to be caused the slightest discomfort, he decided to leave him home. He instructed his other uncles to keep him under their protection and care. The young child watched as preparations for the journey were made but he did not say anything and remained quiet.

At the time of departure, when Abū Ṭālib started to mount his camel, the nephew came forward and caught hold of the camel's nose-string and said in a mournful manner,

"Uncle, you are departing. But with whom are you leaving me?" And while saying this, his eyes were flooded with tears.

These words acted like arrows that upon leaving the child's mouth, pierced through his uncle's heart.

Abū Ṭālib was deeply moved by his nephew's sorrow. He lowered his camel and descending from it, he clasped his nephew to his bosom, kissed him and said,

"No, my son, do not cry! I cannot bear to see you saddened. Come, I will take you with me."

Having said this, he seated his nephew before him on

the camel and left for Syria.

This was the first journey of our Beloved Master[sa].

21
THE OUTCOME OF IGNORANCE

It was in the nature of the Arabian people to continually be occupied in running riots, quarrelling, fighting and killing. They would draw swords on trivial issues and were always ready to take up altercations and battles. Here is an entertaining story about their senseless ignorance.

At a distance of about three days' journey from Makkah was a place called 'Ukāz, where a fair was held every year and where people from all over the country would gather. Business and trading were conducted in abundance, and famous orators, notable poets and renowned writers would display their skills as well. Impressive poems expressing praise called ***qaṣā'id*** (***qaṣīdah*** in singular) would be read and grand intellectual competitions were held. Expert critics would be consulted to decide which poem would be deemed the best of all. The seven best ***qaṣā'id*** were hung inside the Ka'bah and were called the ***saba' mu'allaqāt*** (Seven Suspended Odes).

The king of Hīrah, Nu'mān bin Mundhir, would also send his goods to be sold here in 'Ukāz. He had to take great precautions in sending his merchandise because there was always the danger of it being looted on the way.

One particular year, when he wanted to send his goods to 'Ukāz, he asked while sitting in his court, "Who is willing to take the responsibility of my merchandise?"

At that time, there was present in his court, a man named Barrāḍ bin Qais from the tribe of Banū Kinānah. He was a very devious and cunning man! At the King's query, he stood up and said, "Your Majesty, I will take the responsibility of this merchandise on behalf of Banū Kinānah."

King Nu'mān said, "I fear both Banū Kinānah and Banū Qais. Is there anyone present here in my court who would take charge of protecting my goods from both these tribes?"

Immediately another chief named 'Urwah bin 'Utbah

stood up. He was from Banū Qais. "I accept responsibility for protecting your goods from both the two tribes."

Barrāḍ was filled with rage at this and said, "Do you take the responsibility for Banū Kinānah as well?"

'Urwah replied, "You dog! Don't talk nonsense. Not only do I take the responsibility of protecting this merchandise from these two tribes, but from all the men of the world!"

Barrāḍ was mad with anger! But he thought it was not proper to say anything in the King's presence and remained quiet.

Since 'Urwah had accepted charge of the merchandise, King Nu'mān entrusted him with it and he departed on the journey with his men.

Barrāḍ also left the court and followed, waiting for a chance to exact retribution against 'Urwah. Both continued their journeys simultaneously.

Arriving near Khaibar, Barrāḍ referred to a book of omens in the isolation of the Valley of Taiman, to decide whether he should kill 'Urwah or not. While he was busy consulting this book of omens, 'Urwah arrived by chance and asked him what he was doing.

Barrāḍ replied, "I'm looking for a sign to tell me if I should remove you from this world! Tell me, what do you desire? Should I look for a sign or not?"

'Urwah carelessly taunted him and said, "You would not even dare to throw me a dirty glance!"

At this, keeping a careful watch in all directions, Barrāḍ drew out his sword and very swiftly stabbed 'Urwah in his stomach.

The news of the murder immediately reached the victim's men. They ran after Barrāḍ but he had already escaped towards Khaibar.

Two of 'Urwah's men named Asad bin Jawain and Masādir bin Mālik raced in pursuit of Barrāḍ to kill him wherever he was found and thus avenge 'Urwah's death. Unfortunately, both of these two men did not recognize Barrāḍ by face. They thought that once they reached Khaibar, they would ask around and kill him whenever they had an opportunity.

When they reached Khaibar, the first person they met, was none other than the wretched Barrāḍ himself!

They asked Barrāḍ, "Do you know anything about Barrāḍ? He has recently arrived here."

Barrāḍ replied, "Yes, I do, but why do you ask?"

It seems as if both of these men were extremely foolish. They immediately responded, "He has killed our chief; therefore we have come to kill him."

This put Barrāḍ on his guard. Keeping calm, he answered, "Surely Barrāḍ is most wicked and deserves to be sent to hell with one stroke. A whole world is rebuking him. Both of you should come with me and stay at my place. I will myself take you to the place where he lives and help you kill him."

Unaware of the impending disaster, they both accompanied Barrāḍ, content in their hearts that it had all been arranged so easily. Barrāḍ took them to his house and arranged for their food and lodging. He tied up their camels and supplied fodder. Thus he showed them great hospitality.

He passed one day in entertaining them. The next day he said, "The one who is comparatively braver among the two of you and whose sword is really sharp should come with me so that I can take him to the place where that wretch is hiding."

Masādir said, "I will come with you and Asad will stay here and look after the camels."

Barrāḍ took Masādir and left the city. After passing

through some ruins, they reached a place where Barrāḍ said to Masādir,

"Barrāḍ dwells in the ruin just ahead. Stay here and I will go and check whether he is present or not."

After a while he came back and said, "Yes, he is present and luckily it is a very good opportunity to kill him as he is sleeping. His head can be severed from his body with one stroke. Show me your sword so that I can see how sharp it is."

The innocent and unsuspecting Masādir handed Barrāḍ his sword. Instantly, Barrāḍ attacked Masādir, as suddenly as a cat pounces upon a pigeon, and killed him.

Having done this, he hid Masādir's body and sword among some rocks, then went to his companion Asad and said, "I have never seen anyone more faint-hearted and cowardly than your friend to this day. I took him to Barrāḍ's house while Barrāḍ was sleeping and said to him, 'What are you waiting for? Put him to eternal sleep with one stroke of your sword.' But he was unable to do anything, so I have to come fetch you so that the three of us can finish Barrāḍ off together."

Asad accompanied him and encountered the same fate as his friend.

Having completed this heinous task, Barrāḍ took the camels and left for Makkah.

The Quraish were at the fair in 'Ukāz at that time. While on his way, he sent a man bearing a message for the Quraish, "I have killed 'Urwah. It is quite possible that Banū Qais would want to avenge his death upon you. Therefore, be on your guard."

Barrāḍ had purposefully sent this message to the Quraish since Barrāḍ's tribe, Banū Kinānah, and the Quraish were relatives and friends with each other. It was a common tradition in Arabia that the friend of an enemy was also considered an enemy. In a situation where harm could not be caused to the enemy, the Arabs would seek satisfaction by causing harm to a friend of their enemy instead.

As soon as Barrāḍ's message reached the Quraish, they quickly collected all their men present at 'Ukāz and departed for Makkah, but the news of 'Urwah's murder had already reached Banū Qais. In retaliation for 'Urwah's death the Banū Qais went on a murderous rampage, killing as many men of the Quraish as they could find.

Meanwhile, the Quraish had sought refuge inside the

Ka'bah. The Arabs would never kill anyone who had entered the sacred Ka'bah. Therefore, the Banū Qais returned to their homes saying that 'Urwah's blood would not go unavenged and that the Quraish should be ready to fight them the following year.

Thus the Quraish were forced to spend the entire year in preparation for war.

The following year Banū Qais arrived in Makkah with their ally Banū Hawāzin ready to fight. It was a tradition among the Arabs to cease all fighting during this particular month. But Banū Qais did not take that into consideration and came armed to the teeth with weapons. The Quraish had to enter the battlefield; both of the parties were full of zeal and fervour. Prominent chiefs took oaths that they would rather die fighting than retreat.

Soon a furious battle began to rage and an insignificant argument in the court of Nu'mān bin Mundhir reaped a most catastrophic result. The amount of bloodshed was unparalleled. This battle was one of the bloodiest massacres among the wars of the Days of Ignorance and is known in history as the **Battle of Fijār**.

When the bravest men of both sides were too exhausted to fight anymore and after thousands of men had been wiped out, Banū Qais finally had to admit defeat. They relinquished their right to avenge 'Urwah's death and the Quraish were victorious.

A truce was declared on the condition that the total number of men killed from each side would be counted; and the tribe that had killed more of the other tribe's men would have to pay compensation for those extra men.

After the dead were counted, it was discovered that the Quraish had killed an excess of twenty men from the Banū Qais. Thus the Quraish had to pay compensation for twenty victims and in this manner the two party returned home in peace.

One significant historical aspect of this war is that Abū Ṭālib's sacred nephew also accompanied the Quraish to the battlefield. He was perhaps fourteen to fifteen years old at the time; or according to some accounts, possibly nineteen to twenty years of age. However, all historians agree that this sacred boy neither killed anyone with his own hands nor raised his sword toward anyone. He only gathered the arrows from the battlefield and gave them to his uncles.

This was the first war in which our Beloved Master[sa] participated.

22
THE YOUTH'S PLEDGE

When the people of a nation become tired of tyranny and bloodshed, from among them such individuals arise who strive to stop cruelty and end bloodshed in order to bring peace and tranquility to the world.

This very thing took place in Arabia. For centuries the Arabs had engaged in confiscating others' wealth, devouring the rights of the weak and providing for themselves by causing bloodshed.

When this situation had crossed all limits, a few kind hearted and noble-minded people from among them recognized that a great injustice was being perpetrated. They realized that the entire nation was falling into a pit of devastation and ruin. The strong were devouring the weak and the weak were buried under the oppression of the powerful. Hundreds of homes were destroyed due to frequent civil wars, looting and plunder. Thousands of children were being orphaned. The whole country was in danger of utter destruction. They became determined to liberate the people from their life of cruelty, hardship and oppression; and bring them peace.

Some of the most influential and commanding chiefs from among the Arabs, including Fuḍail bin Ḥārith, Fuḍail bin Wadā'ah and Mufḍil bin Fūḍālah, gathered together and made a pact to stop all cruelty, injustice and excess from that day forward. They decided to use their power to stop anyone from being cruel to the weak; to help the oppressed; to assist the one whose rights had been usurped; and to expel from Makkah any person who continued to be cruel and unjust to others.

Since the names of most of those taking the oath had ***Faḍl*** in them, that event was named as ***Ḥilful-Fuḍūl*** (the 'Covenant of Faḍl) and is known in history as such.

As almost all of the prominent chiefs of Makkah had

participated in this pact, and had shown much enthusiasm when taking the oath, the helpless, and weak people of the city began to expect that they would be saved from the hold of oppressors.

But the condition of Arabia had become so loathsome and offensive, and the attitude of the people had become so base and twisted, that this pact proved to be as short-lived as a bubble. A few days later no one remembered the pact nor did they remember their oath.

When a great number of people were killed in the **Battle of Fijār**, people were reminded of the forgotten pact. Some noble men from among the Quraish desired to revive the Pledge of Fuḍūl and to once again take oaths from people for supporting the oppressed and assisting the weak.

Zubair bin 'Abdul-Muṭṭalib was the one to make this proposal. 'Abdullāh bin Jad'ān was considered to be the oldest and most respected noble man in Makkah at that time. This historic assembly of the Quraish took place at his house.

Banū Hāshim, Banū 'Abdul-Muṭṭalib, Banū Asad, Banū Zuhrah and Banū Tamīm were all a part of this convention. After some enthusiastic and motivating speeches, all present vowed that they would stop the oppressor from being cruel forthwith; assist the person wronged in getting back what was rightfully his; and help the oppressed. Among this assembly of seasoned elders and chiefs of the nation, was a youth who also took the oath.

Unfortunately, within a few days, the elders had already forgotten their promise and their pact. However, that young man remembered his oath very well and dedicated his entire life to fulfilling his pledge. As long as he lived, he strived to his utmost to help the oppressed and sympathize with the helpless. When he departed from this world, he left behind thousands of devout servants who made supporting the vulnerable the purpose of their lives. When tested, they did not even take into consideration the status of a king if it clashed with the interest of a mere rustic peasant!

This young man was our Master[sa].

23
ṢĀDIQ AND AMĪN
THE TRUTHFUL AND THE TRUSTWORTHY

As this young lad grew older, so did he progress in piety and forbearance. No one had ever seen him engage in frivolous activities nor had anyone heard him tell a lie. He was always straightforward in all his dealings and conducted business affairs in an easygoing and excellent manner. Gradually, his reputation of being trustworthy and honest spread all over Makkah. In fact, people began to address him as ***Ṣādiq*** (the Truthful) and ***Amīn*** (the Trustworthy). He was universally respected due to his piety; he also held a high status in the hearts of older and wiser men.

Upon reaching adulthood, he adopted his ancestral profession of trade. However, as he did not possess much wealth, he began by partnering with other people. Thus he began travelling to places like Syria, Baṣrā, Bahrain, and Yemen with his merchandise.

All those who joined him in business during these times had not even the slightest complaint against him and his forthrightness and reliability were never in doubt.

Once a man named 'Abdullāh wanted to conduct some business with this young man. While the mutual discussion was being carried on, 'Abdullāh remembered some other urgent matter and said, "Please stay here. I have to go for an important task; I will settle my affair with you when I return." The young man answered, "Alright, I will wait for you."

'Abdullāh left and forgot that he had asked the young trader to wait for him. Three days later, by chance he passed by the same area and found that noble young man waiting for him at that very spot! He immediately recalled his promise and begged forgiveness for the suffering he had caused saying that he had absolutely forgotten. At this, the young man replied very gently that he had been waiting for him for three whole days.

Our Beloved Master[sa] was given the titles of ***Ṣādiq*** and

Amīn when he was still a young man. Both these titles were a clear proof of what the Holy Quran says about his character:

...فَقَدْ لَبِثْتُ فِيكُمْ عُمُرًا مِّنْ قَبْلِهِ ۖ أَفَلَا تَعْقِلُونَ ۝١٧

Sūrah Yūnus, 10:17

This verse means that when the Holy Prophet[sa] spoke to his people after prophethood, he said, "I have spent a large part of my life among you. Did any of you ever doubt my chastity, my piety, my honesty, and my trustworthiness during that time? When I have spent my youth with such chastity and honesty, would I then, upon becoming older, lie about God? Do you not possess the wisdom to understand such a simple fact?"

If his people did not consider him to be honest and upright, why would they give him the title of ***Ṣādiq*** and if his people did not find him perfect in justice and trustworthiness, why would they address him as ***Amīn***?

24
A PROSPEROUS LADY

There lived in Makkah a prosperous lady belonging to a very noble family. Her name was Khadījah[ra]. She was highly respected throughout the city and there was no one richer than her in all of Arabia.

She was an accomplished trader. She would send people with her merchandise to be sold to places like Egypt, Syria, and Yemen.

When Khadījah[ra] learned about the skill, honesty, and excellent manner of young Muḥammad[sa] in conducting business, she called him and said, "I want you to take my goods to Syria for trading. I will give you twice the amount I pay others for the merchandise being sold, and will send a slave of mine with you to serve you during your travels."

Our young trader accepted these terms and, accompanied by a slave named Maisarah, departed for Syria with the merchandise. When Muḥammad[sa] reached Baṣrā, which is a city to the North of Arabia and South of Syria, all the goods were quickly sold there and at a great profit too! Since he did not have to travel any further, he returned and gave Khadījah[ra] a detailed account of every cent. Then taking what was due to him, he returned home.

Khadījah[ra] inquired of her servant, Maisarah, "Tell me how were your travels and how did this young man of Banū Hāshim treat you?"

Maisarah replied, "My mistress! He turned out to be a unique human being. I have never before witnessed such a well-spoken, virtuous, honest and reliable young man. His treatment of me was like that of a brother. Instead of my serving him, he would be doing tasks for me! He is not a human being, but a complete angel!"

25

MARRIAGE

Ḥaḍrat Khadījah[ra] was as honourable and pure as she was rich and wealthy. Due to her virtue, piety and good morals, she was known all over Makkah by the title of ***Ṭāhirah***.

She was a widow. Her two husbands had passed away and she had decided not to remarry.

Owing to the high character, excellent morals and likeable habits of Khadījah[ra] many noble and respectable chiefs of Makkah had requested her hand in marriage but she had refused them all. Yet upon seeing the wisdom, nobility, and excellent moral values of young Muḥammad[sa] and after listening to his praise from her slave Maisarah, she sent a proposal of marriage to Muḥammad[sa] through her trusted female servant named Nafīsah.

Nafīsah approached Muḥammad[sa] and said, "At your age most men have already fathered many children; yet you have not married. What is your plan with regard to marriage?"
The young man replied, "I am a poor man with limited means of income. Who would give his daughter in marriage to me in such circumstances? After marriage, how will I fulfill the needs of my wife when it is difficult for me to meet my own expenses?"

Nafīsah responded, "In that case you should marry a rich woman. In this way you would not have to shoulder her burden."

The young Hāshmī laughed and said, "Why would a rich man give his daughter to a poor man like me? It is the way of the world that the rich give their daughters only to sons of rich men."
Nafīsah answered, "What if a rich woman desires to marry you of her own will?"

Surprised, the young man asked, "Which rich woman would want to marry a poor man like me?"

Nafīsah replied, "My mistress Khadījah[ra] desires to marry you and has sent me to you with a proposal, provided you are agreeable to it."

The young man said after careful consideration, "What

opinion can I have concerning this? My Uncle, with whom I live and who is my guardian, should be consulted in this regard."

Upon this Nafīsah said, "It is useless to ask Abū Ṭālib unless you are inclined towards it yourself."

The young man said, "No, that is not the case. If my uncle accepts this proposal, I will not decline."

Nafīsah said, "Then you should ask your uncle about this matter. I will come again later to ask you about it."

After Nafīsah left, the young man related the whole affair to his uncle. His uncle said, "If Khadījah[ra] herself is desirous, then you should marry her. Khadījah[ra] is not a stranger; she is related to you as your paternal cousin."

The young man also consulted his other uncles and all of them were of the opinion that the proposal was most appropriate and suitable.

Nafīsah returned in the evening and asked, "Have you spoken to your Uncle?" The young man replied, "Yes, I have spoken of the matter to him and he is agreeable to the match." Nafīsah was pleased and said, "That is excellent! This blessed ceremony should take place as soon as possible since it is not proper to delay something good."

Thus, the details were settled within a few days and Muḥammad[sa] went to the house of Khadījah[ra]'s house with his uncles and other nobility of Quraish. The dowry was fixed at 500 dirhams. Abū Ṭālib performed the ***Nikāḥ*** and thus the marriage was solemnized.

O Khadījah[ra]! May thousands upon thousands of blessings be upon you! You are that fortunate and sacred lady who had the honour of becoming the first wife of our Beloved Master[sa].

The marriage of Khadījah[ra] and Muḥammad[sa] was an exemplary one due to its purity and chastity. At the time of the ***Nikāḥ*** Khadīja[ra] was forty years old and her husband was twenty-five years old. Ḥaḍrat Khadījah[ra] did not think that she was demeaning herself among her tribe and people by marrying a poor man. Her only consideration was her husband's piety and virtues. On the other hand, young Muḥammad[sa] paid no heed to the fact that he was marrying a much older woman despite his own youth. He only considered his wife's nobility of character. As a result of their good intentions, this marriage proved to be an extremely blessed one.

26
THE MOST LOYAL WIFE

At the time of her marriage, Khadījah[ra] considered her husband to be a pious and chaste person. Since she herself had a noble disposition and was inclined towards goodness, she did not choose her husband from among the rich men of her tribe. Rather, she selected a person who, though not wealthy in worldly goods, possessed an abundance of wealth in piety and righteousness.

She had personally experienced his dependability and integrity. However, her young husband's excellent morals were just a small part of his character. Ḥaḍrat Khadījah[ra] was not aware of the innermost merits and virtues that were hidden in his person.

Now that they were living together in the same place she began to realize that her sacred husband possessed a unique personality and virtues that had no parallel.

It was beyond the imagination of Khadījah[ra] that from among the dark particles of Arabia could arise a full moon whose light would, when the time came, spread throughout the whole world. There can be no doubt of the good fortune of Khadījah[ra] whom Allah, out of his extreme Beneficence, granted this abundance of wealth in a miraculous manner.

When the inner perfections and excellences of her husband were revealed to Khadījah[ra] after her marriage, she recognized that there was no other human being in the world who possessed the high, unmatched standard of morals as her husband Muḥammad[sa].

Appreciating this, she began to consider herself the most fortunate woman in the world, which indeed she was!

Khadījah[ra] immersed herself completely in obedience to her esteemed husband, having viewed his conduct and habits quite closely. She set such a grand and chaste example of love and devotion that it stands as a beautiful model for all pious women. With absolute and unshakeable faith, she discovered that though there may be imperfections even in the purest form of gold, there were no defects in her dear husband. He was as distant from sin and transgression as East was distant from West.

Khadījah[ra] was the richest woman in all of Makkah. When she became fully aware of her husband's excellent qualities after marriage, she collected her entire wealth and laid it at the feet of her life-companion and avowed to him that all the wealth was his and he could spend it in any way he desired.

Had young Muḥammad[sa] been fond of seeking pleasure and enjoyment or had he married Khadījah[ra] out of greed for her wealth, it was the perfect chance for him to spend this money on merrymaking. He could have held song and dance parties, done rounds of drinking alcohol, worn the finest clothes, partaken of rich, gourmet food, engaged a large group of male and female servants to serve him day and night and thus he could have spent his life in luxury like a king.

Contrary to all this, he spent all the wealth which his loyal wife had presented to him in aiding orphans, assisting the poor, looking after widows and in taking care of the sick. He would treat his guests well and be most hospitable towards travelers; no beggar left his door empty handed. He would provide clothes to those who didn't have any, feed the hungry, pay debts of those under debt, buy and set free slaves who were oppressed by cruel masters and fulfill the needs of the needy. Yet his life was extremely simple and unceremonious. He did not eat food of high quality, nor did he adorn himself with precious clothes; he did not have slaves to serve him nor did he have a luxurious lifestyle.

His conduct was sympathetic towards all the inhabitants of Makkah. He helped anyone and everyone. If ever there were a quarrel between two people, he would gently moderate the situation and bring them to reconciliation. People had such faith in his trustworthiness that they would give him their possessions to keep and would travel on business to distant lands completely free from care. It was inconceivable that even a penny in the goods entrusted to his care would be lost. People would appoint him as mediator in their affairs; he would always settle their differences with absolute fairness and justice and would never side with anyone unnecessarily.

Khadījah[ra] would observe these virtuous qualities and would be grateful in her heart at God having granted her a husband who had no match and was unique among hundreds of thousands!

She not only loved, but adored her husband, who possessed

angelic qualities and this adoration continued to increase until the time death separated her from her beloved husband[sa].

27
CORNERS OF A SHEET OF CLOTH

One year, there was a flood in Makkah that damaged the walls of the Ka'bah so much that they were on the verge of collapse.

Since the Quraish considered the Ka'bah to be sacred, they first decided to demolish it to the ground and give it a solid reconstruction. At the same time they were wary of demolishing it, in case it brought some curse or bad luck to them. So they could not find the courage to destroy it after all.

Walīd bin Mughīrah, father of Khālid[ra] (Saifullāh) was a noble chief of Quraish. He was extremely old and almost nearing his death. He decided that since he was about to enter his grave anyway, he should start demolishing the Ka'bah. If he died in the near future, it would not make any difference to him. But if he survived, then his people would understand that demolition of the Ka'bah could not bring any punishment.

So he picked up the spade and started striking down the Ka'bah. He continued this till the evening, while being watched by his people.

That night, all of the inhabitants of Makkah kept awake, waiting for God's wrath to strike Walīd down due to his impudence and insolence! But in the morning, they found old Walīd hale and hearty, standing in the Ka'bah's courtyard, smiling at them! The experiment had been a success and the Quraish joined in the demolition. After it had been completely torn down, they started rebuilding it. Each tribe of the Quraish considered it an honour to take part in this task. Instead of laborers, the noble chiefs themselves hauled stones and started the reconstruction.

Among this nobility of the Quraish, was also present that young Hāshmī who was to later become the best of the Messengers, the best of humankind and ***Khātamun-Nabiyyīn***, the Seal of the Prophets.

The work was progressing quite smoothly and the nobility was participating in it with much enthusiasm when there occurred an incident that could have killed the entire population of Makkah and drenched the walls of the Ka'bah with blood!

What had happened? There was a sacred stone called ***Ḥajarul-Aswad*** (the Black Stone) which was fixed in the wall of the Ka'bah. When it was time to put it back in its original place, the chief of every tribe declared that he alone would fix the sacred stone in its place and none dare take away the honour from him.

What would have happened after that? Within moments, all of Makkah was engulfed in the dispute! Like angry lions, each tribe was enraged beyond control. Throwing aside the bricks, cement, and stones with which they had been working thus far, they took out their swords and got ready to kill or be killed. They filled bowls with human blood and took oaths, dipping their fingers into it, to either get what was rightfully theirs or to continue fighting until the last child of their tribe was dead!

Such a frightful incident had never taken place before in the history of the Ka'bah. Every person of the city could foresee streams of blood flowing in the streets of Makkah with dead bodies floating in them. Had a single sword been raised, the entire country would have become engulfed in war and the whole population of Makkah would have been completely wiped out.

Sensing the dangerous situation, some older men tried to

mediate, but none of the tribes were ready to give up their right. Their swords were ready to come out of their sheaths and the arrows in their quivers were prepared to rip through bosoms!

This quarrel lasted four days but no decision could be reached.

On the fourth day, after careful consideration, one chief named Abū Umayyah bin Mughīrah came up with a proposition. He suggested that the first person to enter the Ka'bah early next morning would make the decision to end the quarrel and everyone should accept that without any objection.

"We accept", "We accept", everyone shouted and all began counting the moments to the next morning with great eagerness.

By Allah's design, the first person to enter the Ka'bah the next morning was none other than the grandson of the Chief of Quraish, Āminah's precious gem, 'Abdullāh's darling child, and the husband of Ḥaḍrat Khadījah[ra].

Faces lit up with profound happiness upon seeing Muḥammad[sa]. They shouted with joy, "He is ***Ṣādiq***, he is ***Amīn***. We accept his decision."

The house of Hāshim was happy beyond measure that one of them had earned the honour. The pride of Banū Hāshim, Muḥammad[sa], stepped forward, took off his cloak (in those times, it was a straight sheet of cloth), spread it in the courtyard of the Ka'bah and placed *Ḥajarul-Aswad* on it with his own blessed hands.

Then, addressing the gathered chiefs, he asked all of them to hold the sheet of cloth by its corners and edges.

In accordance with the command of their young mediator, the chiefs of the Quraish held the corners with much fervour and raised it. The young mediator directed, "Still some more, still some more", and the chiefs of Quraish continued to raise it higher.

When the cloth had reached the point in the wall where the stone was to be fixed, then he, who was to become Mercy for all the Worlds[sa], picked up the stone with his own blessed hands and placed it where it belonged.

In this way, because of the young man's foresight, wisdom, and peace-making ability, the fire of revolt was extinguished instantly, which would have otherwise engulfed all of Makkah. The Ka'bah walls would have been left standing, *Ḥajarul-Aswad* would have continued to lie on the ground, but not a single man in Makkah would have been left alive.

This was the first public decision made by our Beloved Master[sa].

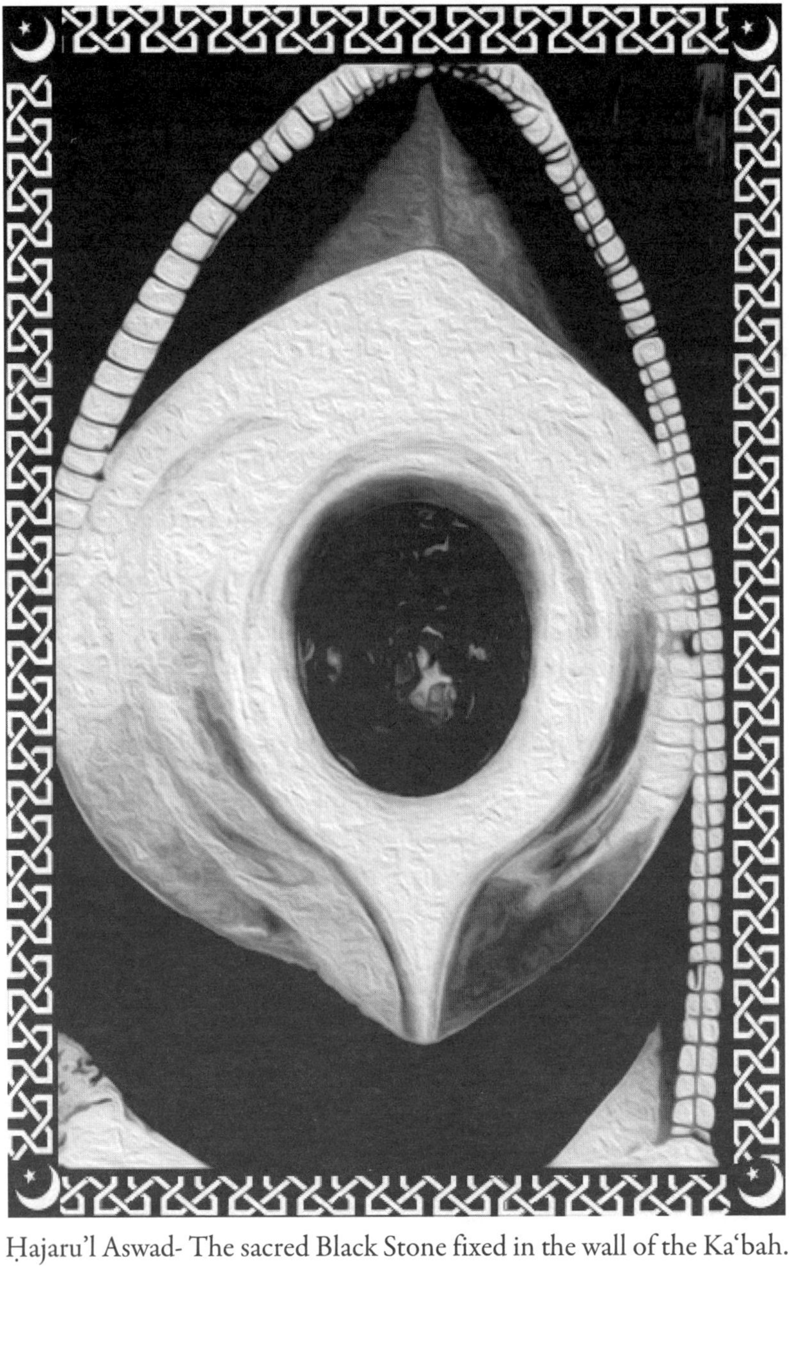

Ḥajaru'l Aswad- The sacred Black Stone fixed in the wall of the Ka'bah.

28
A LOYAL SLAVE AND A BENEVOLENT MASTER

It was a common practice of bandits and highwaymen in Arabia to kidnap children of nobility and sell them as slaves. This very catastrophe befell a respectable person belonging to the Qazā'ah tribe named Ḥārith who was a Christian. His son Zaid was a virtuous and obedient child. He had a charming appearance and possessed attractive habits. He was only eight years old when he accompanied his mother on a journey. On the way, bandits attacked the travelling party and Zaid was taken away with some other children.

As was the custom of those rogues, the children were

brought to 'Ukāz, and sold there. Ḥakīm bin Hizām, who was a chief of Makkah and a nephew of Ḥaḍrat Khadījah[ra], bought three or four boys. Zaid was one of them. Since he seemed more intelligent compared to the other children, the bandits received 400 dirhams in exchange for him.

Ḥakīm bin Ḥizām brought these children home with him. When Khadījah[ra] visited him a few days later, he said, "Aunt! I have bought some slaves a few days earlier and want to present one to you, so please make your selection."

Khadījah[ra] chose Zaid and brought him home.

The child was polite and civilized. Khadījah[ra] said to her honourable husband, "He is worthy of being presented to you; kindly accept him on my behalf."

Zaid was now the slave of Muḥammad[sa].

After his kidnapping, Zaid's mother and father were deeply grief stricken by his separation. They mourned his loss day and night and tears flowed from their eyes incessantly.

The father loved his beloved son immensely; therefore the pain of his loss became unbearable for him. He vented his grief in verses, which said:

"O Zaid! My eyes shed tears at your loss and a string of tears keeps flowing;
But I know not whether you are alive or dead?
Zaid! Where should we look for you; have you drowned in the ocean or has the earth swallowed you?
Would that I could know if I would be able to meet you in this world or not!
As the sun rises each morning, I see you sitting in its sphere;
And as it begins to set, I see your image in the golden twilight of the distant horizon and grow restless;
Each evening, when the moon comes out, I writhe in your memory at its very sight;
And when the stars twinkle in the dark sky at night, I lose my self in imagining you,
When the cold wind blows, it strikes my grieving heart like an arrow;
And when the gust of hot air blows, it turns on the flame of your remembrance in my heart;
I will ride a camel and travel the whole world and look for you in each corner of every country- perhaps I may find you somewhere;
If, due to my bad luck, I find no clue of you, then I will lay down my life searching for you;
And as I approach death in your search, I shall instruct Qais, 'Umar, Yazīd, and Jiblah in my will to give up their lives looking for you."

Ḥārith would ask every person he met, “Have you seen my son anywhere? His countenance is like that of a crane’s feather!”

Whenever he heard of a caravan going to another city, he went to meet those travelling with it and said to them, “If you find my son anywhere, bring him back with you. He is an eight-year-old innocent child. He has an attractive visage and a fine voice!”

Thus passed many years but no trace was found of the one lost like Yūsuf.

Then all of a sudden, there appeared a ray of hope. A few men of Banū Kilāb, upon their return from Hajj, told Zaid’s father, “Your son is the slave of a man named Muḥammad[sa] in Makkah. Somebody must have sold him at his hand. We met your son. He is very happy and comfortable. His master keeps him very well. Upon inquiry, we found that Zaid’s master is a grandson of Abdūl- Muṭṭalib, the chief of Quraish and is a magnanimous, kind hearted, friendly and courteous man. Whomever we met in Makkah praised Muḥammad[sa]. The entire nation has conferred on him the titles of the Trustworthy and the Truthful. Although this man is still very young, every person in Makkah respects him. We are certain that if you go to Makkah and ask Muḥammad[sa] for Zaid, he will surely return your son to you."

Suddenly there was hope in a desperate situation; the light of happiness was illuminated and clouds of hopelessness drifted away. Father and uncle left for Makkah, taking a large amount of money with them. Once there, they sought and reached Muḥammad[sa] and said to him, "O son of the chief of Quraish! O the dearly beloved one of Banū Hāshim! O noble and highly respected young man! We have newly entered this place and have arrived but yesterday. Both at home as well as here, we have heard a lot of praise regarding your high moral qualities and your charming habits. We have come to beg of you and have hope with respect to your noble nature that you will not turn us away disappointed. The fact is that we are dwellers of Yemen. We had a son named Zaid. Bandits caught him and we have heard that he was sold at your hands. O Benevolent One! We implore you to kindly give him back to us. Take as much money as you want in return. We shall pay you without hesitation and will forever remain grateful for your favor."

The Holy Prophet[sa] became worried upon hearing this speech from Zaid's father. Actually, he had begun to love Zaid so much that he did not want to be separated from him. On the other hand he could not bear to keep the boy forcibly with him, separating him from his mother and father. He began to think of how to answer Ḥārith.

Seeing the Holy Prophet[sa] perplexed, Ḥārith said with a great deal of anxiety, "O noble son of the chief of Quraish! We beseech you in the name of your honourable ancestors to have mercy on us and return our boy to us. Would that you realized how the parents are afflicted upon being separated from their child and how restless and anxious they grow upon losing their child. Trust us when we say that we have passed this entire period mourning his loss."

The noble son of the chief of Quraish replied, "That is not the case. I fully realize the grief you must have gone through upon being separated from your child. Your son is surely with me but the fact is that having lived with him for this much time, I have begun to love Zaid so much that separation from him causes me pain. Cannot there be any other means of reconciliation?"

From this discourse with the Holy Prophet[sa], both the brothers thought that this son of the Hāshmī chief did not want to free their son from his servitude and was making excuses to put the subject off.

Thinking this and getting disappointed, Ḥārith said, "What reconciliation and through what means? We cannot think of anything. Tell us yourself how this can be achieved."

The Holy Prophet[sa] replied, "I have thought of a way provided you are agreeable to it. That is to ask Zaid himself concerning this. If he wants to go with you, he surely can. I will absolutely not take any money from you in exchange for him; you may happily take your child back. But if instead of accompanying you, he prefers to stay with me, then I would request you to leave him here if you so will. And rest assured that as long as I am alive, your boy shall not have any kind of discomfort here. But if you do not agree to this, then I do not want to force you; you can take your child with you with pleasure."

Would there be a slave anywhere who would not want to be set free? And would there be a son on this earth who would prefer to live with a stranger rather than his own parents? It is quite obvious that the comfort and luxury a child gets from his parents can never be obtained elsewhere and the degree with which parents can love their son can never be given by anyone else.

Considering this, both the father and the uncle readily

agreed to the young master's proposition and said, "What you have said is absolutely correct and proper. We agree to it and accept it. Surely Zaid should be asked. If he wants to live with you, we shall have no objection. But you should remain faithful to your word. Do not refuse (what you have said) later on. Breaking a promise is not befitting for one of such a noble ancestry."

Instead of getting angry, the young chief smiled at this and said, "To this day, the thought of not fulfilling a promise or turning back on my word has never even occurred to me. Be assured that I shall stay true to my word under all circumstances. Zaid has gone out to play somewhere. You can ask him when he comes back."

While these discussions were going on, Zaid came in from outside in a happy mood. As he was about to enter the interior of the house, his Master[sa] called him, "Zaid! Come here."

Upon hearing the call, Zaid turned around and was stunned to see his father and uncle in front of him.

The Master[sa] said, "Zaid, do you recognize these two men?" Zaid[ra] said, "Yes. This is my father. This is my uncle." Saying this, the young child ran and hugged his father and the father clasped him to his bosom with great love. The uncle, too, kissed him.

Now the Master[sa] asked, "Zaid! These two have come to take you with them. Tell us, what do you wish? Do you want to go with them?"

The father and uncle both looked at Zaid[ra] with immense fervour to see what Zaid's[ra] reply would be. They were amazed beyond bounds when contrary to their expectation Zaid[ra] replied, "I shall stay with you – I do not want to go back to my home and shall not go at all."

At this his father said with amazement, "Zaid[ra], do you prefer slavery over freedom? If such is the case, then I greatly lament your wisdom!"

Zaid[ra] answered, "Surely I prefer slavery to Muḥammad[sa] a thousand times above freedom. The merits and virtues I have witnessed in the person of my honourable Master[sa] have not only enslaved my body, but my soul as well forever. I shall leave the company of my Master[sa] only when I die."

At this spirited display of the slave's loyalty, the Master[sa] took hold of his hand with excessive affection and took him to the Ka'bah. Father and uncle accompanied them.

There were some noble men of the Quraish present inside the Ka'bah, talking amongst themselves. Having reached their presence, the young Master[sa] said, "Those of you, who are present here at this time, bear witness to the fact that from today, I free Zaid[ra] and adopt him as my son. He shall inherit from me and I shall inherit from him."

The father and uncle stood next to them. It was beyond their imagination that a boy could leave his parents and feel proud at being the slave of another person and also that a master could treat his slave with such mercy and compassion.

For both the brothers, this display of affection and love on one hand and of sympathy and compassion on the other was wondrous. They were completely amazed and could not believe that such masters and such slaves existed in this world. When they realized that the boy was not willing to go with them under any circumstances, they went back, leaving him behind.

Ḥaḍrat Zaid[ra] kept his word to the extent that he laid down his life for his Master[sa], thus setting a seal to the truthfulness of his words and his loyalty. May God shower thousands upon thousands of His blessings on him.

This was the first slave of the Holy Prophet[sa].

Regarding this very slave the daughter of ***Ṣiddīq-e-Akbar***[ra], Mother of the Faithful, Ḥaḍrat 'Ā'ishah[ra] says that if Zaid[ra] had been alive at the time of the Holy Prophet's[sa] demise, the Holy Prophet[sa] would have given him a part in his inheritance.

What greater proof of the nobility, respect and greatness of Ḥaḍrat Zaid[ra] can there be that from among all the companions of the Holy Prophet[sa], only Ḥaḍrat Zaid[ra] earned the distinction of being mentioned by name in the Holy Quran.

29
THE DAWN OF THE LIGHT OF PROPHETHOOD

Now the dawn of prophethood was close at hand and the time of disbelief was nearing its end. The world that was drowning in a quagmire of sin was about to be reborn to a new life. The satanic powers and evil forces that had taken hold were about to fade away. God's Kingdom was about to be established on the earth as it was in the heavens.

The world that had been full of corruption, persecution and oppression was about to be reborn with justice, faith and belief.

The cloud of darkness that had spread all over the world

was now about to be cleared. The long awaited time had come for God's Mercy to be showered upon mankind. Now, the corrupt people were to be washed clean of their bad deeds. The fire of violence and fury that had been burning in their hearts was about to be replaced with inner peace and tranquillity. The harsh and strict ways that were apparent everywhere in the world were about to be annihilated. The time had come to end the abuse of the weak, the poor and the subordinates. The Blessed Guide[sa], the Leader[sa] was coming to lead the world to the right path; and the Emperor of Both Worlds[sa], at God's command, was about to come forth. He would come with a noble purpose and with a blessed prophethood. The works of Satan, i.e., bad morals, indecency and persecution that were prevalent, were about to be erased. Instead, these would soon be replaced by sincerity, love and brotherhood for all. Indeed, God's majesty was about to prevail in the world.

The world that was without religion and full of idol worshipping was about to be purified. Soon the bleak world would be illuminated with faith, the Oneness of God, and knowledge. Our beloved Prophet[sa] would come and uphold God's command to cleanse the darkness of sin and disbelief, at a time when the world was fully absorbed in vice. Morals had decayed and frivolous customs were prevalent at this time. Importance was placed on every type of idol worship. People were ready to fight and kill each other for the smallest of reasons.

At the time when all of this was common practice, the Holy Prophet[sa], the Mercy for the entire world, came and changed the state of the affairs in an astonishing way. The change that he brought about was dramatic and has been described as follows:

If there were no ugly and dark face for comparison,
How could anyone appreciate the beauty of the beloved?

30
THE KING OF IDOLS IN THE HOUSE OF GOD

Ḥaḍrat Ibrāhīm[as], and his son, Ḥaḍrat Ismā'īl[as] built the Ka'bah for the worship of God, and God alone. However over the course of time the children of Ḥaḍrat Ibrāhīm[as] and Ḥaḍrat Ismā'īl[as] turned away from worshipping God and began to worship idols. They became so engrossed in these pagan customs that they turned away from the One True God and filled the Ka'bah with idols. Over time the number of idols began to increase until there were three hundred and sixty idols! Indeed it is likely that there was no house of idols that contained as many idols as those within the Ka'bah.

The king of the idols within the Ka'bah was called ***Hubul*** and had been placed upon the roof of the Ka'bah. It was because of this idol, ***Hubul***, that the worshipping of idols became the practice across Arabia. At that time the responsibility of looking after the Ka'bah belonged to Makkah's powerful and influential Prince, 'Amr bin Luḥaiyy, who belonged to the tribe of Khuzā'ah.

Once Prince 'Amr bin Luḥaiyy became extremely ill and despite trying numerous remedies his ailment was not cured. Someone told him that there is a spring in a place called Ma'āb in Syria. He heard that by bathing in the water of that spring his illness would be cured and he would be restored to good health.

Accordingly, Prince 'Amr bin Luḥaiyy went to this spring, bathed in the water, and was cured. During his stay in Ma'āb, he observed that the people living there were worshipping idols and bowing down to them. For Prince 'Amr bin Luḥaiyy this was a sight that he had never before witnessed. He was astonished to see such a practice. Out of curiosity he asked the people, "Why are you bowing down to these and who are they?"

The people of Ma'āb replied, "Sir! Do you not know? Let us tell you that these are extremely useful figures! They fulfil all of our needs whatever they may be. They provide for us! They may look just like stones, but in reality, they are extremely powerful! When we need rain, they provide rain! When we need sunshine, they provide sunshine! They demolish our enemies! They keep our friends happy and they keep us content. They even make us better when we are ill and free us of debts! In fact, whatever we ask of them they provide it!"

Upon hearing these agreeable words Prince 'Amr bin Luḥaiyy impulsively said, "If this is the case then you people are in the right place! If you could be so kind as to give me one of these idols, I will take it back to my country. You will not miss but one idol, but for my people and I, it will create such ease!"

So the people of Ma'āb decided that they would give the Prince one of their idols. The idol given to Prince 'Amr bin Luḥaiyy was none other than ***Hubul***. The Prince took ***Hubul***, a stone, back to Makkah and proudly placed this stone upon the roof of the Ka'bah. Prince 'Amr bin Luḥaiyy began to go around Arabia, house to house, telling the people about ***Hubul*** and inviting them to worship it.

Prince 'Amr bin Luḥaiyy was a very influential and generous person and people felt indebted to him for all he had done for them. In light of this they obeyed him and began worshipping the idol. Over time, the Ka'bah became the central point for idol worshippers.

31
IDOL WORSHIPPERS

The Ka'bah was the central point for worship in Arabia and everyone had immense respect for the Ka'bah. Idol worship eventually spread throughout Arabia. In fact, it became so prevalent that every family and household had their own god!

All of these idols were unfinished and shapeless stones. When a person went on a journey he would take three stones with him. Over the course of the journey, wherever the traveller stopped, he would use the stones to make a fireplace for cooking. When he was done with his meal, he would take one of the same stones and prostrate in front of it. This tradition was common in the middle phase of idol worshipping.

When idol worship became deeply rooted in Arabia, the Arabs did not even need to take three stones with them on journeys. During a journey wherever they stopped, they would just pick up any stone out of their pocket, worship it and then put it back in their pocket.

Strangely, even though they were devoted to these stone idols, when they were unhappy with a situation they would curse at these very same gods! The story of Imra'ul-Qais, a very famous poet tells more about this practice. It was very unfortunate that someone killed Imra's father. This naturally saddened him a great deal. Imra decided to ask his idol to guide him in whether to take revenge for the killing of his father. People would draw lots to see what the idol wished to say. The idol told him that he should not take revenge.

The poet became very angry but thought maybe the draw of the lot was not right, as an idol cannot be so unjust. He decided to pick another stone. But yet again the draw of the lot showed that revenge should not be taken. Now the poet lost control and became very angry. In his rage he spat at his god and said, "How dare you! If your father had been killed, then I'd like to see you not taking revenge!"

There is another account of how people would so easily disrespect their so-called gods. There was a man whose camel was ill. He took the camel to his idol and requested that the camel's health be restored. The idol was called Sa'd. As it so happened, upon seeing the idol the camel became frightened and immediately ran out of sight!

Upon this the man spoke with great anger, "You cursed idol! What kind of an act did you just pull? Tell me, now what am I supposed to do and where am I going to find my camel? Who made you Sa'd? You are just bad luck!" Saying this, he slapped the idol across its face, which broke off the idol's nose!

In the same way that they would get angry at their idols when things were not in their favour, they also had great love for these lifeless idols. Every day they would witness dogs come and urinate upon their idols, but it did not change the love they had for them. Many times people would come and leave food as an offering in front of the idol. The dogs would come, eat a free meal and would be on their way with their tails wagging. People would see this but it would not reduce the love they had for their gods.

Another story that illustrates the absurdity of worshipping

idols concerns a person named 'Amr bin Jamū'. 'Amr bin Jamū' made an idol out of wood so that in case of an emergency he could worship at home at his own convenience. In his neighbourhood there were two men, Mu'ādh bin Jabal and Mu'ādh bin 'Umrah. While 'Amr bin Jamū' was away from home, they would often creep into his house and throw the idol into the latrine.

When 'Amr bin Jamū' returned, was upset that his god had been dishonoured in such a way. With great love, he would pull his god out of the filth, wash it with water, dry it with a cloth, put perfume on it and return it to its place. This mockery would take place daily, but the two neighbours would not stop their mischievous ways, nor would poor 'Amr bin Jamū' stop believing in his god.

Along with love, Arabs would also have great fear of their gods. There was a boy who was given some milk, a bit of butter and some cheese by his mother and was told to go and give it to their idols. Upon seeing the fine quality food and drink, the boy's mouth began to water. He was tempted to eat it all by himself and just tell his mother that he gave it to the idols. But he also feared that the idols might get angry at this act and break his neck. What would he do? The boy could not work out how to solve this problem, and so unwillingly and with anger he took the milk, butter and cheese and placed them in front of the idols while his mouth was still watering. Not long after that a dog showed up. He drank the milk and ate the cheese and butter, after which he urinated upon the idols!

Once an interesting incident took place with one of the idols. The idol was called *Ḥais* and was made solely from dates. Whenever there was any gathering in the town, people would bring dates and pile them up. Over time, a huge pile of dates was created and every day the idol became both taller and wider. In fact *Ḥais* was becoming fatter and fatter every day. However something occurred that ended up ruining the life of poor *Ḥais*. It so happened that in Arabia a great shortage of food and drink occurred. So much so, that there was nothing left for the people to eat or drink.

People sincerely prayed to their idols asking for rain. But it neither rained nor did the famine come to an end. Out of starvation, the people became desperate for their lives. As was the tradition, the elders of the tribe got together to try and find a solution to their problem. They finally came up with a plan that involved the end of *Ḥais*. They decided that in order to get rid of their hunger, they should eat ***Ḥais***! As soon as they had made this decision everyone charged towards ***Ḥais,*** and whatever dates came in hand they grabbed and ate them up! Within seconds the idol was eaten up and the floor where he once stood was left spotless!

32
SAVAGE PRACTICES

The people of Arabia were inveterate idol worshippers, but along with this they were also exceptionally stubborn, great troublemakers and proudly uneducated. Their behaviour often came across like that of savage animals, so much so that there was no one like them anywhere in the world! Over trivial matters, they would exact bloodthirsty vengeance that would go on for years upon years. This would lead to the death and annihilation of tribes upon tribes and thousands of men. These fights were over petty matters that would cause laughter in an educated person. For example, once while a camel was eating, it wandered into someone else's field. At that time, by chance, a lady was looking after the fields. She hit the camel and chased it out of the field. The owner of the camel was furious and he began beating the lady causing her to be severely injured.

The lady called for her people, while the owner of the camel called for his people. Both sides pulled out their swords and began fighting. Slowly, it escalated with some people joining one side and some joining the other. This progressed into a war! The fight began between two families, but over time, many other Arab families became involved in the war. This war dragged on for forty years and ultimately claimed the lives of seventy thousand people. Only after countless years of death and bloodshed was the anger in the hearts of these people finally quenched and the war came to an end. A famous poet of India, Maulānā Ḥālī, says about this war:

> *The fight of the tribes of Bakr and Taghlab that annihilated tribes upon tribes*
> *Half a century was wasted and due to this a war spread across Arabia.*
> *The fight was not over money, nor the nation, but only due to being uneducated.*

There is another instance of the inhabitants of Arabia getting into petty quarrels. Once there was a horse race taking place. The horse, whose name was Dāhis, was about to take the lead in the race when a troublemaker scared the horse. This action led to a war that lasted not for one or two years, but for a total of sixty-three years in which many tribes were completely destroyed and killed.

A person from the tribe of Banū Kinānah took a loan from a man of the tribe of Naḍar. After asking for repayment a number of times, the person that gave the loan took a monkey to a fair that was called 'Ukāẓ . He stood in the middle of the fair and said:

I sell this worthless monkey, because of the debt owed to me by a person from the tribe of ***Banū Naḍar****. Is there anyone who will buy this monkey from me?*

The people of Banū Naḍar did not like this at all. One person from the tribe of Banū Naḍar crept up behind the monkey and dealt him a powerful blow with a stick. The blow was so powerful that the monkey fell to the ground and died instantly. Immediately, swords were drawn from both sides and the tribes prepared to fight and die. If not for the intervention of wise elders, the fairgrounds would have become a battlefield. Through dialogue, luckily a war was avoided and both sides began to calm down. Otherwise so much blood would have been shed that day that there would have been streams of blood flowing.

Once there was a tall and heavy person by the name of Tarīf bin Tamīm who was performing *Ṭawāf* of the Ka'bah. While performing the *Ṭawāf* he could not help but notice that a person by the name of Hamīsa bin Jandal was looking at him very closely. Tarīf stopped doing the *Ṭawāf* of the Ka'bah and asked, "Brother, what is your problem? Who are you? And why are you staring at me with such intensity as if you want to do me harm?"

Hamīsa said in reply, "Indeed, my intention is something like that! If we ever come face to face in battle, I will most certainly blow this giant melon head of yours off! If your life is precious to you, then watch out!"

Hearing this Tarīf became full of anger and immediately raised his hands in prayer and said, "O ***Hubul***! O king of the idols! Be so kind as to enable me to compete with this evil man this year, so that I can place this rejected head in front of you as an offering."

Hamīsa did not hold back either! He also said in a bold voice, "O ***Hubul***! O lord of all strength and powers! You are not just the lord of this wretched person, but you are my lord as well! Make me triumphant over this dog this year, so that I can throw the dead body of this loathsome being into the jungle for the jackals to enjoy!"

Imagine how many people must have endured witnessing this ridiculous exchange of words between these two men!

There was a person by the name of Baḥīr. He was standing in the fairgrounds watching the crowds go by, when someone called Qa'nab came up in front of him. Baḥīr asked him, "Qa'nab, where has that horse of yours gone, which was called Bayzah?" Qa'nab replied, "Where would she be? She is with me, but what is it to you? Why are you asking about her?"

Baḥīr said, "I'm asking because this was your only horse that flew like the wind, because of which you were saved from my hands. Otherwise you would have been killed by me long ago!" Qa'nab said in great confusion: "What are you talking about? When has there ever been a competition between the two of us? When was I riding away from you on my horse? This is a complete utter lie! Get lost from here you devil!"

Upon this both prayed, "O ***Hubul***, whoever is the liar and disbeliever should be killed by the one who is the truthful." Prior to this short, yet heated conversation, there were no ill feelings between them. However, after this day, they became enemies and thirsty for each other's blood. Finally, a day came that Qa'nab the owner of the horse that ran like the wind, murdered Baḥīr.

Within Banū Ṭā'ī there were a number of tribes who had feuds against one another. Ḥārith bin Jabalah Ghassānī was someone who sought to make peace between all those who were fighting. Unfortunately, his efforts were in vain and peace lasted for just a short time. One day, without any reason, Banū Judailah attacked Banū Ghauth. The leader of Banū Judailah, Asba', was killed in the fight. A person by the name of Maṣ'ab cut off the ears of Asba' and used them to patch the holes in his shoes. He then read a couplet:

We sew our shoes with your ears and fill your skull with wine and eat with pleasure from it.

There was a person from the tribe of Banū Ẓafar, by the name of Rabī', who used to buy camels and take them to his town. Once he was on his way going about his daily business, when he crossed paths with a person from the tribe of Banū Najjār who was sitting outside his home. Upon seeing Rabī', he called out, "Who are you? Where are you coming from and where are you going?" Rabī' replied, "I'm not going to tell you, and who are you to ask this of me? Tell me why are you asking me where I am going? What right do you have to ask me this?" Upon saying this, in one stroke Rabī' cut off the man's head. The result of this barbaric behaviour was a horrific war that began between Banū Ẓafar and Banū Najjār.

This next account shows the extent of ignorance of the Arabs. It is quite barbaric and shocking beyond belief! While sitting around without any provocation, a thought came to the leader of the tribe of Banū Biyāḍah, 'Amr bin Nu'mān. He said to his tribe, "The place where we live is not worth living. There is a shortage of water, there is a shortage of grass, there is seldom grains for food, there are no fields, the air and water is bad, the whole area is wretched!

"In comparison, the lands of Banū Naḍīr and Banū Quraizah are extremely favourable. They are extremely green and lush, the air and water is clean and fresh, water is readily available, and food is readily available for the animals. Why should it be that they live in ease and we put up with hardship? In no way are those people any better than us! So what right do they have over that land? Go and tell them straight away that they should hand over their land to us immediately, otherwise we will capture and kill forty of their boys!"

When this message reached the people of Banū Quraizah and Banū Naḍīr they were very surprised. For the sake of their children's lives, they decided that they should leave their homes and give whatever properties they had to Banū Biyāḍah as demanded.

As they were preparing to leave, a person from the tribe, Ka'b bin Asad, said to them, "Why worry about the children, they can be born once again! Once you leave your land you will never get it back. So let the children be killed, but whatever you do, don't leave your land." The people of the tribe agreed with what he was saying and sent a message to Banū Biyāḍah saying, "Kill our children if you want, we will not leave our lands!"

When the message from the two tribes reached Banū Biyāḍah, the brutal 'Amr bin Nu'mān captured the innocent children of the two tribes and butchered them in an extremely savage manner.

Upon this a great and bloody war began in which thousands of people were killed. Mischievous and immoral conduct was a common practice for these people and it would be on display at every given opportunity. Serious issues and conflicts were created due to their capricious nature, but they would not stop their senseless behaviour.

There was a person by the name of Ḥāṭib bin Qais. A person from the tribe of Banū Tha'labah came to him as a guest. Ḥāṭib took his guest to a bazaar, called Sūq Banū Qainuqā'. At that time there was a big troublemaker by the name of Yazīd bin Ḥārith. Upon seeing the guest, Yazīd realised that he was from another town. He wanted to do something disruptive and said to a Jew, "If you go and kick that outsider really hard in the back I will give you my shawl right here on the spot!"

The Jew was ready to do so, but he said that he would do it only if he got the shawl before he did it. Yazīd took off his shawl and handed it over saying, "Here, now let the show begin!" The Jew slowly crept up behind the outsider, and upon seeing a chance, kicked him in the back so hard that the poor guest narrowly escaped falling flat on his face.

When people saw this, they began to laugh and joke about it. They got great entertainment from this. The guest called Ḥāṭib to help him. When Ḥāṭib heard what had happened he became enraged and lost control. He picked up his sword and chopped off the head of the Jew!

Yazīd heard about what happened to his friend and he came after Ḥāṭib in order to exact revenge for the Jew. He attacked Ḥāṭib with his sword, but Ḥāṭib managed to escape. However, in Ḥātib's tent there was a person from another tribe Banū Mu'āwiyah. When Yazīd was looking for Ḥāṭib and went into his tent, he saw that person and said to him, "If Ḥāṭib runs away it does not matter, because I can take my revenge on you instead. Indeed, it looks as though you are sitting in his place!"

Although this person from the tribe of Banū Mu'āwiyah didn't even know what had happened, Yazīd attacked him without mercy. Soon, the innocent man was lying dead on the floor. As a result of this, such a savage war began between the two tribes that one can only beg of God's forgiveness!

During the war some people tried to make peace be tween the tribes and they even said that from both sides whatever damage has been caused they would take care of the repairs. But the cruel and unjust leaders of Aus, 'Amr bin Nu'mān, and Khazraj, Ḥaḍīr bin Samāk, didn't accept this. It was only when thousands of men from both tribes had been killed, many women widowed, hundreds upon hundreds of children left orphaned, did the war finally come to an end. This war has gone down in the history of barbaric people as 'The War of Ḥātib'.

33
SACRIFICE OF MORALS AT THE ALTAR OF IGNORANCE

The habits of the Arabs of the time were extremely crude. Some of their habits defied reason and the traditions they followed were nothing short of ridiculous. Reading and writing was thought of as a sin and considered the work of servants. They were proud to live without education and they saw those that could read and write as lower class citizens. In the eyes of respectful and decent people, there was nothing worse than one of their people knowing how to read or write!

Despite this, something inspired Ḥaḍrat 'Umar[ra] to secretly learn to read and write from a servant. However, he tried to keep this private so that no one would find out he was learning to read and write. It so happened that one of his friends knew about this so-called "bad habit" and came to him. He said, "I've come to you at this time for a very important matter. I need you to write a letter to a person who lives in Yathrib (ancient name for city of Madinah). A group is going there, I will send the letter with one of the men."

Ḥaḍrat 'Umar[ra] responded, "How can I do such a job? If I write this letter for you then my life will be in danger and I will become ridiculed by the whole population. Go from here now!" The friend said, "Sir, who will know whether you have written it or if a servant has written it? Please write it! My need will be filled and it will be of no harm to you."

Ḥaḍrat 'Umar[ra] replied, "Absolutely not! This is very risky. By no means am I ready to get involved in this dangerous job. If a person even hears a whisper that I had anything to do with writing the letter, then I will not be able to show my face again in this town. Is it the work of a decent person to read or write?"

The friend said with false praise, "Sir, come on, just write it! If I wasn't desperate then I would never push for you to do it."

Ḥaḍrat 'Umar[ra] finally gave in and said, "All right, if you insist then I will write it, but on the condition that you give me your word that you will not tell a single soul that 'Umar[ra] wrote this letter for you. If anyone hears that I did it, I will be ridiculed for no reason." The friend gave his solemn promise and swore by Hubul that he would not tell anyone that Ḥaḍrat 'Umar[ra] wrote it. Only then did he write the letter.

The wild behaviour of the Arabs was so audacious that they would rob during broad daylight and would steal from guests and then kill them. Most disturbing of all is that it did not bother them in the slightest to kill and shed blood at the slightest provocation. In fact they would proudly mention it in poetry. Before the bloodshed they would openly discuss where they should commit robbery, what tribe should be looted and by which means they steal the property and animals from others.

Maulāna Ḥālī wrote about them in the following words:

The character of all of them was that of wild animals, and every person was just as one in robbing and killing
All their time was spent in stirring trouble; there was no law and order
They were so skilled at robbing and killing, like animals are fearless in the jungle.

Pride, arrogance and falsehood were so much a part of their nature that they were completely consumed in it. They would go to the graves of their elders and they would proudly boast, "See here! This is our elder, who was extremely strong and brave. If you ever had such a person among your elders then show us his grave. Otherwise, go hide your face in shame and go drown yourself in a few drops of water!"

When such challenges were given, the people would no doubt get angry and once again the fighting and terror would start.

So shameless were the people that they would do the *Ṭawāf* of the Ka'bah naked and would say that when we were born from our mother without clothes, then what wrong is there in doing the *Ṭawāf* naked?

They were so immoral that one woman would marry ten men at the same time and when she felt like it she would divorce all or a few of them. Similarly, men were also accustomed to having as many wives as they wanted. Not only would they have as many wives as they pleased, men also often exchanged wives with their friends. They didn't even see anything wrong with marrying two sisters to one man at the same time.

One extremely shameful custom of the time was that if a father had numerous wives and the father died, then apart from their blood mother, the son could marry whichever of their step mothers they wanted to.

When a woman's husband would die, she would remain secluded at home for one year. The conditions of the seclusion period were spent in the strangest of ways. Old, dirty and smelly clothes would be worn and the woman would sit in the smallest and darkest room in the house with an extremely low ceiling. During this period of a full year she would neither wash, nor change clothes, nor cut her nails, nor put on any perfume. After a year had passed, a donkey would be brought to her with which she would scrub her body. After that camel's dung would be brought to her. The lady would stand and hold out her hands, upon which the camel dung would be placed. The woman would throw the dung over her shoulders. With this event, the period of isolation would come to an end.

The property of a son's parents would only go to those who excelled in robbery and murder and were able to compete without fear against their enemies! Women, girls, and little children wouldn't inherit anything from their fathers. They would drink alcohol so extensively that one could not even force oneself to drink that much water! They were stingy beyond belief, but for alcohol, they would spend with open arms and would be proud of it. There would be alcohol parties everywhere, which would be held with great honour. Glass after glass would be freely consumed. Alcohol was so prevalent that they would shower it over the graves of their relatives and friends as a sign of love. Apart from pouring alcohol over the graves they would also keep the graves wet with the blood of camels and horses.

Gambling was seen as an extremely pure and blessed hobby. If a man did not gamble, he would be seen as contemptible and would be hated by others. Those who did not gamble were not respected by their relatives nor their tribe, and such a person would be shamed everywhere. While gambling they would lose their wealth, but not only this, they would also gamble away their wives.

When a person was about to die, they would state in their will that people should cry and wail. So, accordingly, all the women from the family would get together at the deceased man's house. They would undo their hair, put ashes in it and then would begin wailing extensively. They would make such a ruckus that it would create havoc and it would be heard all over the neighbourhood. During the wailing, they would slap their own faces and would rip their shirts open. Women that were closely related would also shave their heads. When the funeral procession would be taken towards the cemetery, they would hire paid women to do the wailing. All the relatives, men and women, would walk behind the coffin with bare feet.

When they returned from the burial, they would gather together with great pomp and would serve food and celebrate. This ritual would be repeated on the third, tenth, twentieth, and fortieth day, of the person's death. The same would occur after six months and on the first anniversary. If the deceased were a person that was well known and generous, they would tie a live female camel to the grave. This was done by digging a very big hole in which the camel could stand. Then they would stand the camel in the ditch by twisting the camel's neck to such a degree that it would face towards the camel's tail and they would tie all four legs to the neck with ropes. Then leaving the camel in this torturous position they go home. They would not give the camel anything to eat or drink and often the poor camel would die in that position.

35
ABSURD CUSTOMS

The thoughts and beliefs of the people of Arabia were also extremely peculiar and again were stranger than anywhere else in the world. For example, in a year that there would be no rain, they would take a few cows, attach some sticks to their tails and set the sticks on fire. Then they would take them to the top of a hill and upon arriving there they would pray to their idols for rain. They also believed that every person has a snake living in their stomach. When the snake would bite the person's ribs and liver it would make the person hungry!

If a person suffered psychological problems they would say that a filthy ***Jinn*** has entered that person. The treatment for such a person would be to tie either dirty clothes or smelly bones around their neck. They would believe that by doing this the unclean spirit would leave the person's body. Snakes were thought to be the friends of ***Jinn***. They believed that if a snake were killed, then a ***Jinn*** would definitely take revenge. Before the ***Jinn*** could take revenge, they would quickly hide the dead snake in the manure of animals.

For the treatment of women whose children would die at birth, the lady would have to cross over the body of a dead man with her feet in such a manner that the body of the dead man became distorted. They believed that by doing this the ladies illness would be cured. When a brave enemy would attack them, and they were not able to compete against his strength, then their women would go and sit in the middle of the battlefield and would urinate. Their belief was that by doing so, the battlefield would become flooded and the fire of the war would be put out.

If a person from a particular tribe called Badawī tribe had the good fortune to own one thousand camels (which was a huge amount of wealth in those days) they would poke out the eye of one of their camels to keep away bad luck. This would blind the camel in that eye and they would have no regard for how painful this would be for the camel and how it would scream with pain. When a person would gain another thousand camels, then he would poke out the other eye also, making the camel completely blind. Like this, by making one camel useless, they thought that the rest of the camels would remain safe.

When someone would get a fever, he would take a rope and tie it to a tree and would believe that whoever unties this rope will catch the illness from him and that he would become cured from it. One of their most mischievous and awful superstitions was that when a person would be killed, an owl would come out of the head of the dead person (which they called ***Hāmmah***). This owl would call out, 'Revenge, revenge!' throughout the woods.

It would then become obligatory upon the relatives of the person that was killed, to kill the person who had killed their relative.

When they managed to kill the person, then ***Hāmmah*** would come out of this dead person's head and it would fly around in desolate areas calling out in a terrifying voice 'Revenge, revenge!' And finally, when the relatives of the victim would kill the person who murdered their relative, an owl would come out of the head of that person and it would bellow from the top of the mountains and would shout, 'Revenge, revenge,' in the most fearful of voices.

Like this, ***Hāmmah*** would come out of whoever had been killed and the owl would fly around in the air shouting, 'Revenge, revenge!' When revenge had been taken, then the owl of that person would die. And whoever's revenge wasn't taken or couldn't be taken, that tribe's owl would remain in the valleys, flying around saying 'Revenge, revenge!' The worst part about this belief was that it was unending. Upon killing someone, revenge had to be taken and this kept carrying on! The fire to take revenge remained on going within the tribes. If someone wanted to tease the other tribesmen as cowardly, they would say, "What mouth can you show in front of us, the owls of your relatives are still flying around in the valleys," meaning that you are so cowardly you can't even take revenge for your dead relatives.

34
A TERRIFYING SCENE

Arabia was the centre of many evil practices, but the harshest of most heinous of all was the common practice of killing their innocent daughters. This tradition was so horrific and heart breaking that when one reads the accounts, it defies belief how cruel and savage these people were.

There were various ways of killing girls. The most common practice was that when a girl reached the age of five or six, the father would go to the woods, dig a deep hole and return home. He would then wash his daughter and dress her nicely, put perfume on her, and then he would take her into the woods. Over there he would stand her by the edge of the hole and would say to her, "Look down, what do you see?" When she would look down, the father would give her a hard push from behind and would start to fill the whole with mud until the ground was flat once again.

Some people would get their daughters ready in the same manner and would take them to the top of a mountain and from there they would throw the tiny and precious life down. There were also those men that would tie stones to the waist of their daughters and then drown them in a spring.

Other times, when a girl would be born, they would immediately take her to the woods and would bury her alive. For those men who did not want to take their daughters to the woods and bury them alive, they would say to the mother to hold the girl by both legs and the head. They would slaughter their daughter themselves and bury her in their yard.

In some cases it would be the mother herself that would kill the daughter. In regards to this Maulānā Ḥālī said,

Whatever daughter that was born to a house,

The fearful yet merciless mother

When watching her husband's expressions of killing their daughter,

Then she herself would kill and bury their daughter alive.

She emptied her lap in such a way,
As if someone had given birth to a snake

After the advent of the Holy Prophet[sa], a new convert to Islam asked him, "Ḥuḍūr, how will our sins be forgiven? Before the advent of Islam, we committed such traitorous and colossal sins. I had a daughter, who was so beautiful and innocent. She loved me with all her soul and would always be with me. Whenever I would come home, she would run and cling to me. Sometimes she would lie down in my lap; sometimes she would climb on my shoulders. She would say such sweet things that even strangers would fall in love with her.

When she turned six, I dressed her in new clothes, in which she looked like a beautiful doll. I said, 'Come with me.' Upon this she happily and laughingly started walking along with me. I took her to a well, and when I was about to push her in she cried out, 'Father! What are you doing? I will fall.' I didn't care about what she had said, and gave her a hard push. She fell in the well and died instantly."

Upon hearing this horrific account, the Holy Prophet[sa] cried so much that the whole of the Holy Prophet[sa] beard became wet with tears.

Similarly, another man told the Holy Prophet[sa] about the killing of his daughter, "My daughter was just two years old when I decided to bury her alive. I took her to the woods and when I started burying her, my daughter held on to the corner of my clothes with her tiny hands. I yanked her off my clothes and quickly filled in the hole. Until I finished flattening the ground, I could hear her calling out to me, 'Father! Father!' from within the hole."

How did this cruel tradition come to Arabia? Nu'mān bin Mundhir the King of Hīrah, to whom they paid their taxes, ruled the people of Banū Tamīm. But later the people of Banū Tamīm became rebellious and stopped paying their taxes to King Nu'mān bin Mundhir. King Nu'mān bin Mundhir sent his brother in command of some of his army and they marched towards the tribe. They took many of the lambs, goats and camels as well as many of their women.

Afterwards, the tribes became very remorseful and sent the leaders of the tribe to King Nu'mān bin Mundhir to ask forgiveness for their transgressions, to pledge loyalty to him and to pay their dues. When King Nu'mān bin Mundhir forgave them, they asked for their flock and women to be returned to them. Nu'mān bin

Mundhir returned the animals. However, he decided that while the women were free to return if they so wished, if any of them wanted to stay they would not be forced to leave.

One of those ladies was the daughter of Qais bin 'Āṣim. Qais sent his son-in-law to bring back his wife but she refused to return. She wanted to stay with the man who had originally captured her. When the father heard of this, he was appalled at his daughter's choice and he swore that if any other daughters were born to him, he would bury them alive. After this, he had twelve or thirteen daughters, all of whom were buried alive.

Over time, this practice began to spread. So much so, that many of the Arab tribes became accustomed to this terrible act. How heart breaking, how shameful and how scary a sight this must have been, when a father buries alive his own flesh and blood! This tradition vividly illustrates the fact that the people of Arabia were by far the most cold hearted and shameless in the world.

36
LIGHT IN THE DARKNESS

What you have read is just a snapshot of the treacherous ways of Arabia at the time. Not only Arabia, but also the whole world was in a similar state at that time. The neighbouring country to Arabia, Iran, was absorbed in fire worship and people were immersed in enjoying themselves in every type of immoral conduct.

India was rooted in the worship of thousands upon thousands of idols and they considered themeselves superior to the whole world. Yet the state of the people known as 'the Untouchables' in their own country was worse than that of dogs! Brahmins (the upper caste) considered themselves like gods and believed that the whole country belonged to them and that everything was under their authority. The whole of China, a vast country, was heavily steeped in the belief of nature and spirits. They also had idols seated with all their glory. The rest of Asia was also in complete darkness and involved in bad works, in which people lived like wild animals.

In Europe, only Rome and Greece were worth mentioning. They honoured both their heritage and culture. However, both countries were absorbed in idol worship where thousands upon thousands of idols were being worshipped for centuries. The rest of the continent was full of people that lived like wild animals who were always killing and looting. They lived in caves and they drank alcohol out of the skulls of humans.

The only place where there was any sign of decency in their culture and their way of life was in Syria. But even there, the land was full of idol worship and no one knew about God. America and Australia were undiscovered territories at that time, and no one knew of them.

In other words, at that time, there was no place in the world that was not deeply engrossed in idol worship and where homes were not filled with idols, and where every other person had their own god which they worshipped. There was nowhere, that the worship of one God took place. The belief in God as the Living; the Self-Subsisting and All-Sustaining; the Master; The One without any partner; and only worshipping God alone was not apparent anywhere in the world.

They used to say god was mud, fire, water, wind ,
Mountains and rivers, lightening and clouds.
On earth: mud, stones and trees were worshipped,
They even worshipped what was above the skies, the stars,
the sun and the moon.
They asked for their desires to be fulfilled from things
that were worthless;
Nothing was left that could be worshipped, except God.

The disbelievers and wrongdoers had reached their absolute limits. The whole world was buried in the worship of all elements beyond belief and to such an extent that it was difficult to pull them out. God the Almighty wanted His Creation to come out of this dark abyss that the world had become; and for people to recognise the Strong and Mighty God, the true Master and Creator of all the world.

Then, with absolute mercy upon the mankind God sent

the Holy Prophet[sa], who came and removed the total darkness in which the world was entrenched. The veil that had been placed over God's shining light was removed; upon seeing which the pious people fell down in prostration. The one who came and showed the right way, the revered Holy Prophet[sa], the guide, the teacher, the beloved, upon him we send thousands of salutations of peace.

> *My body and my soul for you I sacrifice, by your birth, man*
> *was brought back to being civil and you saved their dignity.*

37
THE BLESSED CAVE

Upon observing the filthy and impure state of the world, the man who was eternally pure, both inside and out, would be heart broken. He yearned for people to reject satanic acts, and rather lead a pious and clean life. He would constantly think of ways to change things, but nothing would come to mind that could change the state of the world. His heart began to dislike this evil world and he began to be afraid of living in the company of these beast-like people.

Three miles from Makkah, at the top of Mount Ḥirā, there was a cave. The Holy Prophet[sa] would take food and drink for five or six days and he would go to this cave. Here, he would contemplate in peace and quiet, thinking about what could be done to turn things around, and reform the nation.

At times, the Holy Prophet's[sa] loving and caring wife, Khadījah[ra], would go with him. Both husband and wife would cry in the cave for the sake of the nation, contemplating how to bring the nation back to the straight path. They would pray for it, and would remain busy in thoughts of God.

This lasted for a very long time, but the Holy Prophet's[sa] sorrow and sadness would not go away. However, during that period the Holy Prophet[sa] had many dreams that came true. Some of the dreams often came true right away. This was the beginning of his prophethood.

38
THE ANGEL OF REVELATION

One day the Holy Prophet[sa] was sitting in Cave Ḥirā as was his daily routine, when suddenly a sharp light similar to lightening came before his eyes. The Holy Prophet[sa] raised his eyes, and what did he see? It was a gloriously pure being, full of brilliant light, sitting on a throne between the heavens and the earth. Radiant illumination surrounded his majestic throne.

This was the heavenly angel that came to the Holy Prophet[sa] with the first message from Allāh. His name was Ḥaḍrat Jibrīl [Gabriel], who is also known as ***Rūhul-Qudus***, 'the Spirit of Holiness'.

The Holy Prophet[sa] saw Ḥaḍrat Jibrīl and became apprehensive and awestruck. The angel came down in all his glory and stood before the Holy Prophet[sa]. The angel's face was incandescent and rays of light were illuminating the atmosphere. The angel said: "Muḥammad! Read." The Holy Prophet[sa] responded with fear, "I have not been educated."

Upon hearing this, Ḥaḍrat Jibrīl moved forward, held the Holy Prophet[sa] and embraced him close to his chest. Then he let go and said again, "Now read!" The Holy Prophet[sa] gave the same answer, "I have not been educated."

The angel once again held the Holy Prophet[sa] close to himself and pressed him hard against him and said, "Now read!" The Holy Prophet[sa] once more gave the same reply that he had given twice before. After this, the angel sent by God, held him close to his chest again and said the following:

بِسۡمِ اللّٰہِ الرَّحۡمٰنِ الرَّحِیۡمِ ﴿۱﴾
اِقۡرَاۡ بِاسۡمِ رَبِّکَ الَّذِیۡ خَلَقَ ۚ﴿۲﴾
خَلَقَ الۡاِنۡسَانَ مِنۡ عَلَقٍ ۚ﴿۳﴾
اِقۡرَاۡ وَ رَبُّکَ الۡاَکۡرَمُ ۙ﴿۴﴾
الَّذِیۡ عَلَّمَ بِالۡقَلَمِ ۙ﴿۵﴾
عَلَّمَ الۡاِنۡسَانَ مَا لَمۡ یَعۡلَمۡ ؕ﴿۶﴾

In the name of Allah, the Gracious, the Merciful.

Convey thou in the name of thy Lord Who created,

Created man from a clot of blood.

Convey! And thy Lord is Most Generous,

Who taught man by the pen,

Taught man what he knew not.

Sūrah al- 'Alaq, 96:1-6

The Holy Prophet[sa] read these words along with the angel, after which, the angel vanished. This was the first revelation that was bestowed upon the Holy Prophet[sa].

39
A STEADFAST AND DEVOTED WIFE

The incident that took place in the Cave Ḥirā was a new and surprising encounter for the Holy Prophet[sa]. Due to the tight embrace of Ḥaḍrat Jibrīl, the Holy Prophet[sa] began to sweat and he became intensely worried. He was confused and did not comprehend what was happening, or what was to come. The Holy Prophet[sa] came out of Cave Ḥirā in a state of extreme anxiety and headed home.

The Holy Prophet's[sa] caring wife, Ḥaḍrat Khadījah[ra], saw her husband's face and she began to worry. She stood up immediately and said, "My dear, my life is sacrificed for you, what has happened? God forbid, are you not feeling well?"

The Holy Prophet[sa] was shaking and his heart was beating very fast. "*Zammilūnī, zammilūnī* (put a cloth over me, put a cloth over me)," Ḥaḍrat Khadījah[ra] swiftly took off her shawl and placed it over her beloved husband. She sat close by him and began to massage his body.

For some time they stayed in this state. When he began to feel some relief, his wife asked him gently, "What happened and why are you feeling so distressed?" The Holy Prophet's[sa] heart was still beating fast, "Tell me quickly what the matter is, my heart is filled with worry by seeing you in such a state," said Ḥaḍrat Khadījah[ra].

The Holy Prophet[sa] said "Khadījah[ra]! Whatever I have seen and whatever has confronted me today, you will not believe it."

Khadījah[ra] spoke, "My dear husband, tell me what happened? Why will I not believe? To this day you have never said anything that I have not believed."

The Holy Prophet[sa] told her, "Today, as I sat as usual in the cave and was immersed in prayer, all of a sudden, a bright light flashed before my eyes. As I looked up, I saw a spiritual being floating between the heavens and the earth. I was looking at it in astonishment, when he came down and embraced me three times while reciting some verses to me, which I still remember now. After that, he suddenly vanished and darkness overcame the cave. I began to fear for my life.

The Holy Prophet[sa] had just said this when his worried wife immediately responded,

"No, no! Do not even think like that. Allah the Almighty will never waste you! You treat people with the utmost respect; you speak the truth and always walk on the right path; when people are in need, you come to their aid. The good moral values, that have become extinct these days, are all present within you. Your hospitality of guests is always with an open heart. In every good work you help people. So how is it possible that Allah the Almighty would waste such a pious person? You must not worry in the slightest.

As far as today's incident is concerned, it may well be surprising and also startling, but there is no need to worry. I will take you to my cousin, Waraqah bin Naufal. He is extremely knowledgeable about religious scriptures. He will surely be able to give us a satisfactory explanation of today's happenings and the incident. Do not worry. You should eat some food and get some rest first. When you are feeling a little better we will both go together to Waraqah bin Naufal."

40
A WONDROUS EVENT

Just before the sun comes up, the early dawn brings a very pure white light, which shows that the night is ending and a new day is beginning. In the very same way in the land of Arabia, as the dark night of idol worshipping was about to come to an end, some intelligent and righteous people were about to be awakened. As they rubbed their eyes to awaken, they realised that the thousands of idols that they had been worshipping were nothing but stone that could neither speak, nor listen, nor could they come to anyone's help, nor could they protect anyone, nor could they get rid of anyone's worries. Although their inner purity told them that these idols were nothing, their current state of mind was unable to show them the true path towards Allah the Almighty. This path to Allah could not be seen without the pure light and guidance of Allah.

Those people, who had become fed up and left idol worship, were but a few. One was Zaid bin 'Amrū, the other was known as Qais bin Sā'idah and another one was named 'Uthmān bin Ḥuwairith. But out of all those that had left idol worship, the most renowned was the prominent Waraqah bin Naufal. He had left idol worship and had become a Christian.

Waraqah bin Naufal had mastered the meanings of the Old Testament, the Book of Zabūr and the New Testament, as well as the prophecies of those prophets that had passed before and their religious scriptures. Within the Quraish, Waraqah bin Naufal was very well respected. Khadījah[ra] took her husband to Waraqah bin Naufal and said "Cousin, today a very strange happening took place with my husband. I want you to listen to his account and tell us what this means." The elderly Waraqah bin Naufal said "Sir, tell me what happened?"

The Holy Prophet[sa] explained, "Today I was in Cave Ḥirā remembering God, when I saw a very magnificent being that came down from the sky and while embracing me said 'Read'. After that he recited a few verses to me and then vanished into thin air. That is all."

Waraqah bin Naufal listened to the whole account carefully. He then asked, "Do you remember the verses that he recited to you?"

The Holy Prophet[sa] answered, "Yes, I remember them very well." After that the Holy Prophet[sa] recited all the verses that had been revealed in the cave.

After listening to the verses Waraqah bin Naufal said, "Muḥammad, you are the most fortunate person, I give you glad tidings of being a Prophet and Messenger. The being that you saw was that very same angel that Hadrat Mūsā[as] [Moses] saw. The verses that he recited to you, I swear to you by God, they were words that came from God Himself. If I live until such a time that you are driven out of here by your country, then I will most certainly come to your aid. By God I pray that I stay alive until that time, but the odds are against me as I have become very weak and old. My hands and feet no longer work and my hearing is fading. It is possible that I have between six months to a year of life left.

After hearing what Waraqah bin Naufal had to say, the Holy Prophet[sa] asked in astonishment, "But why would my country drive me out of here? I have never done anything wrong to anyone! I care for all and want the best for everyone. Everyone is happy with me, there is not a single person in the whole of Makkah that is against me or is my enemy. So I do not understand why my country would drive me out? No, this cannot be! This can never be! What have I done wrong for my countrymen to want to send me away?"

The old man smiled and said, "O Prophet to be! This will not make any sense to you right now! But the fact of the matter is that whenever such a revelation comes to a person, that person is severely persecuted and tortured by his very own country; so much so that at the end he is driven out. God be with you and may He protect you from the enemies."

This was the first person to affirm the prophethood of the Holy Prophet[sa].

اقرأ باسم ربك

PUBLISHERS' NOTE

The following abbreviations have been used. Readers are urged to recite the full salutations when reading the book:

sa ṣallallāhu 'alaihi wa sallam, meaning 'may peace and blessings of Allah be upon him,' is written after the name of the Holy Prophet Muḥammad[sa].

as 'alaihis-salām, meaning 'may peace be on him,' is written after the name of Prophets other than the Holy Prophet Muḥammad[sa].

ra raḍiyāllahu 'anhu/'anhā/'anhum, meaning 'may Allah be pleased with him/her/them,' is written after the names of the Companions of the Holy Prophet Muḥammad[sa].

In transliterating Arabic words we have adopted the following system established by the Royal Asiatic Society.

ا	at the beginning of a word, pronounced as a, i, u preceded by a very slight aspiration, like h in the English word honour.
ث	th, pronounced like th in the English word thing.
ح	ḥ, a guttural aspirate, stronger than h.
خ	kh, pronounced like the Scotch ch in loch.
ذ	dh, pronounced like the English th in that.
ص	ṣ, strongly articulated s.
ض	ḍ, similar to the English th in this.
ط	ṭ, strongly articulated palatal t.
ظ	ẓ, strongly articulated z.
ع	', a strong guttural, the pronunciation of which must be learnt by the ear.
غ	gh, a sound approached very nearly in the r grasseye in French, and in the German r. It requires the muscles of the throat to be in the 'gargling' position whilst pronouncing it.
ق	q, a deep guttural k sound.
ء	', a sort of catch in the voice

Short vowels are represented by:

a for ـــَــ (like u in bud)

i for ـــِــ (like i in bid)

u for ـــُــ (like oo in wood)

Long vowels by:

ā for ـــاــ or آ (like *a* in *father*);

ī for ى ـــِــ or ـــِــ (like *ee* in *deep*);

ū for و ـــُــ (like *oo* in *root*);

Other:

ai for ى ـــَــ (like *i* in *site*);

au for و ـــَــ (resembling *ou* in *sound*)

The consonants not included in the above list have the same phonetic value as in the principal languages of Europe. While the Arabic ن is represented by *n*, we have indicated the Urdu ں as *ń*. Curved commas are used in the system of transliteration, ' for ع , ' for ء.

We have not transliterated Arabic words which have become part of English language, e.g. Islam, Quran, Hadith, Mahdi, jihad, Ramadan and ummah. The Royal Asiatic Society rules of transliteration for names of persons, places and other terms, could not be followed throughout the book as many of the names contain non-Arabic characters and carry a local transliteration and pronunciation style which in itself is also not consistent either. All the words that appear in bold italics in the text can be found in the glossary.

The Publishers

GLOSSARY

‘Abdul-Muṭṭalib- Chief of the Quraish, custodian of the Ka‘bah and grandfather of the Holy Prophet[sa].

‘Abdullāh- Father of the Holy Prophet[sa].

Abrahah- Christian governor of Yemen who tried to destroy the Ka‘bah.

Abū Bakr- Best friend of the Holy Prophet[sa] and the first Caliph of Islam.

Abū Lahab- The uncle of the Holy Prophet[sa] and his bitter enemy and persecutor.

Abū Ṭālib- Beloved uncle of the Holy Prophet[sa] who raised him after the death of his grandfather.

Abyssinia- Region across the Red Sea from Arabia.

Aḥadīth- Plural of hadith, see Hadith.

Allah- Allah is the personal name of God in Islam. To show proper reverence to Him, Muslims often add Ta 'āla, 'the Most High', when saying His Holy name.

Amīn- Title given to the Holy Prophet[sa] meaning 'Trustworthy'.

Āminah- Mother of the Holy Prophet[sa].

'Ā'ishah- Wife of the Holy Prophet[sa].

Banū/Banī- A tribe or clan.

Banū Hāshim- Most noble tribe of the Quraish. Tribe of the Holy Prophet[sa].

Banū Jurhum- First tribe to settle in area of Makkah.

Banū Zuhrah- A respected Quraish tribe named after the planet Venus. Tribe of Ḥaḍrat Āminah.

Battle of Fijār- A battle fought in the days of ignorance in which thousands died.

Durūd- Invocation of blessings upon the Holy Prophet Muḥammad[sa].

Hadith- A saying of the Holy Prophet Muḥammad[sa] . The plural is aḥadīth.

Ḥaḍrat- A term of respect used for a person of established righteousness and piety.

Ḥajarul-Aswad- The sacred Black Stone fixed in the wall of the Ka'bah.

Hājirah- Ḥaḍrat Hagar[as].

Ḥajj- Pilgrimage to the House of Allah in Makkah, Arabia; also known as the fifth pillar of Islam.

Ḥalīmah- Wet nurse of the Holy Prophet[sa].

Hammāh- Name of an owl from Arab superstition that would demand vengeance.

Ḥilful-Fuḍūl- Pledge of Fuḍūl. A pledge taken after the Battle of Fijār to protect the oppressed. The name Fuḍūl is derived from the names of those who took the oath.

Ḥirā- Name of the cave in which the Holy Prophet[sa] would go to worship.

Holy Prophet[sa]- A term used exclusively for Ḥaḍrat Muḥammad[sa], the Prophet of Islam.

Hubul- Name of ancient idol. King of idols; placed on roof of Ka'bah.

Ibrāhīm- Prophet Abraham[as].

'Īdul-Aḍḥā- Islamic festival commemorating the great sacrifice of Ḥaḍrat Ibrāhīm[as], Ḥaḍrat Ismā'īl[as], and Ḥaḍrat Hājirah[as].

Islam- Peace and submission; Name of religion brought by Muḥammad[sa].

Ismā'īl- Prophet Ishmael[as].

Jibrīl- Archangel Gabriel.

Ka'bah- The first House of Allah, rebuilt by Ḥaḍrat Ibrāhīm[as] and Ḥaḍrat Ismā'īl[as]. Located in Makkah and central to the Muslim pilgrimage of Hajj; Muslims turn towards it when praying.

Khadījah- A wealthy widow who became the first wife of the Holy Prophet[sa].

Khātamun-Nabiyyīn- Seal of the Prophets; Title of the Holy Prophet[sa].

Marwah- One of the two hills between which Ḥaḍrat Hājirah[as] ran in search of water. This act is one of the rituals of Hajj.

Madinah- City approximately 200 miles north of Makkah to which the Holy Prophet[sa] migrated and where he is buried.

Makkah- City of the birth of the Holy Prophet[sa] and location of the Ka'bah.

Maulānā Ḥālī- Famous Indian poet.

Muḥammad- The Holy Prophet[sa] of Islam.

Nikāḥ- The announcement of marriage in Islam.

Qaṣīdah- Traditional Arabic poems of praise.

Qiblah- Direction to face for prayer (Ka'bah).

Quraish- Most highly respected tribe in Arabia.

Quran- Holy book of Muslims, revealed to the Holy Prophet of Islam[sa].

Ruḥūl-Qudus- Name given to Angel Gabriel meaning 'the Spirit of Holiness.'

Ṣādiq- Title given to the Holy Prophet[sa] meaning 'Truthful'.

Ṣafā- One of the two hills between which Ḥaḍrat Hājirah[as] ran in search of water. This act is one of the rituals of Hajj.

Ṣalāt- Formal Islamic Prayer offered according to a prescribed procedure.

San'ā'- Capital of Yemen.

Shaqq-e-Ṣadr- Splitting of the chest. First known vision of the Holy Prophet[sa].

Ṣiddīq-e-Akbar- Faithful witness of the truth; title of veneration for Ḥaḍrat Abū Bakr[ra].

Ṭāhirah- Pure, Virtuous; Title given to Ḥaḍrat Khadījah[ra] due to her piety and good morals.

Ṭawāf- The performance of circuits around the Ka 'bah as a form of worship.

Waraqah bin Naufal- Cousin of Ḥaḍrat Khadījah[ra] who was a Christian and knowledgeable about holy scriptures.

Yathrib- Ancient name for city of Madinah.

Yemen- Region in the south-western part of Arabia.

Zaid- A freed slave and adopted son of the Holy Prophet[sa].

Zamzam- Spring of water that miraculously appeared after the desperate prayers of Ḥaḍrat Hājirah[as].

OUR BELOVED MASTER

محمد ﷺ

Study Guide & Workbook

WHO COULD IT BE?

"The wife was the daughter of the King of Egypt. She had been brought up in a palace amid excessive wealth and fortune. To forsake her would mean her end in merely two days. Who was she? ______________________

"My honourable father! Obey immediately whatever has been commanded. God willing, you shall find me patient and obedient." Who said this? ______________________

"If I have ten sons born to me and they all reach their youth in my lifetime, then I will sacrifice one of them in the name of God." Who said this? ______________________

"She was the daughter of Wahb. She was most virtuous, cultured and of a pleasant disposition. Upon growing up, she was to marry the illustrious son of 'Abdul Muṭṭalib." Who was she? ______________________

"Surely I prefer slavery to Muḥammad[sa] thousands of times above freedom." Who said this? ______________________

"Allah Almighty will never waste you. All good moral values, that have become extinct these days, are all present in you." Who said this? ______________________

"You didn't have any concerns for your Ka'bah which I plan to destroy with such a large army that even if all the inhabitants of Arabia join to fight it, not one of them will leave alive." Who said this? ______________________

Ḥaḍrat Ismā'īl[as]	Abrahah-King of Habash	Waraqah bin Naufal	Ḥaḍrat Hājirah[as]
Ḥaḍrat Āminah	Ḥaḍrat Zaid[ra]	'Abdul-Muṭṭalib	Ḥaḍrat Ḥalīmah[ra]

WHAT HAPPENED FIRST?

Put the corresponding letters in order in the timeline below:

O: Ḥaḍrat Āminah[ra] has a dream in which a bright light comes out of her and spreads all around.

L: Ḥaḍrat Ibrāhīm[as] prays to God that he many be granted a son despite his old age.

E: Ḥaḍrat Ibrāhīm[as] and his son, Ḥaḍrat Ismā'īl[as] rebuild the Holy Ka'bah.

V: The foundation of the city of Makkah is laid.

A: Muḥammad[sa] marries Ḥaḍrat Khadījah[ra].

L: An angel visits Muḥammad[sa] and tells him to recite.

F: 'Abdullāh marries a pious lady from the tribe of Banū Zuhrah.

R: A child is born in the family of Quraish, and he is given the name "Muḥammad."

O: Ḥaḍrat Ibrāhīm[as] leaves his infant son and his wife in the desert.

L: Waraqah bin Naufal tells Muḥammad[sa]: "The angel who descended upon Moses[as] has descended upon you."

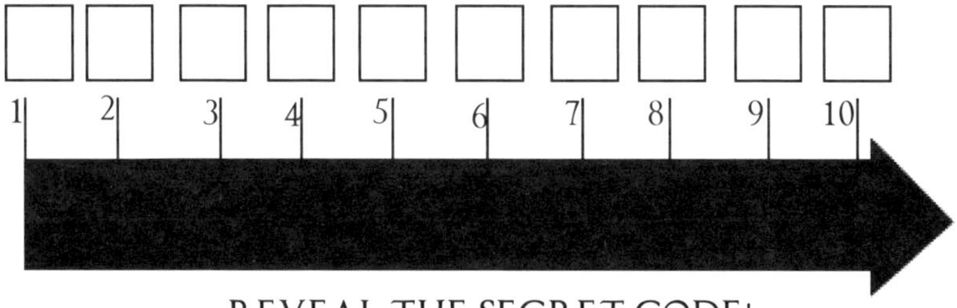

REVEAL THE SECRET CODE!

CROSSWORD

ACROSS

2. Son of the Prophet Ibrāhīm[as]
4. A city in Arabia
5. Name of the angel that came to the Prophet Muḥammad[sa]
7. Wet nurse of the Prophet Muḥammad[sa]
9. The first mosque
11. Father of the Prophet Muḥammad[sa]
12. The Truthful

DOWN

1. The sacred Black Stone fixed in the wall of the Ka'bah
3. Mother of the Prophet Muḥammad[sa]
6. The Trustworthy
7. Prophet Muḥammad[sa] belonged to the tribe of_______.
8. King of the idols of the Ka'bah
10. Divine Spring

WORD SEARCH!

Use the clues below to find the correct words.

```
M Q B N C K T L Z V M M J P A N K D P L
A Y Z U M I A G P Q O H L P V Q A F B A
K X A G E L B X E U F L J N J V B Q K B
K J Y A P S R D J R P S F B R S A C A D
A L J R M G A R I A D W G K X I H V H U
H J M H K R H D P I Q V O S O D A G A L
A E I O A L A C X S R P W U Y K B Q S M
D G R W T L H P X H O X C Z C M G J H U
T T X R T V I S O U Z Y Z P R H Y R I T
Q S U N Q K J M V V T Y H A E A W U M T
W J M U I D U L A D H A V M M M Q U A A
F H L J F D M H I H V U P X P Z B M J L
X A B U L A H A B L K S J L J M A N W I
M U J L M J E X Z U H R A H R K T M L B
D G V N W A T Q F N F E V B D H A J J Q
```

Clues:

1.) The water spring which laid the foundation of Makkah is known as_____.
2.) The Muslim pilgrimage to Makkah is called_________.
3.) The Islamic festival that reminds Muslims of the sacrifice of Ḥaḍrat Ibrahim[as] & Ḥaḍrat Isma'il[as]?
4.) The mosque that Ḥaḍrat Ibrāhīm[as] and Ḥaḍrat Ismā'īl[as] reconstructed.
5.) Where is this mosque located?
6.) 2500 years after Ḥaḍrat Ibrāhīm[as], who were the most respected people in Arabia?
7.) The Chief of Makkah and the custodian of the Ka'bah.
8.) The name of the Prophet Muḥammad's[sa] tribe.
9.) The name of the Prophet Muḥammad's[sa] mother's tribe.
10.) "Though I have brought your child back, I have grown to love him so much that I don't want to be seperated from him; I will be most grateful if you grant me the favor of letting him stay with me for some more time. Who said this?
11.) The name of the governor of Yemen who planned an attack on the Ka'bah.
12.) The name of the uncle of the Prophet Muḥammad[sa] who later turned into his arch enemy.

FILL IN THE BLANKS!

1.) Abū Ṭālib would constantly be amazed at the _______________ and _______________ habits that his nephew possessed.

2.) Abū Ṭālib loved his nephew very much and couldn't bear to see him ____________.

3.) Ḥaḍrat Muḥammad[sa] developed a ___________ for useless parties and functions from an early age.

4.) In the first war that Ḥaḍrat Muḥammad[sa] was a part of, he _________killed or raised a _____________ to anyone.

5.) The pledge that was taken to help the weak and helpless people of the society was called the _______________________________.

6.) Some elders promised that they would protect the weak and helpless from hardship, cruelty and oppression and grant them _____________________.

7.) As a youth, Ḥaḍrat Muḥammad[sa] took part in his pledge and___________________ to give all his help to the weak and oppressed.

8.) ____________________ was the only member who fulfilled his pledge until the end of his life.

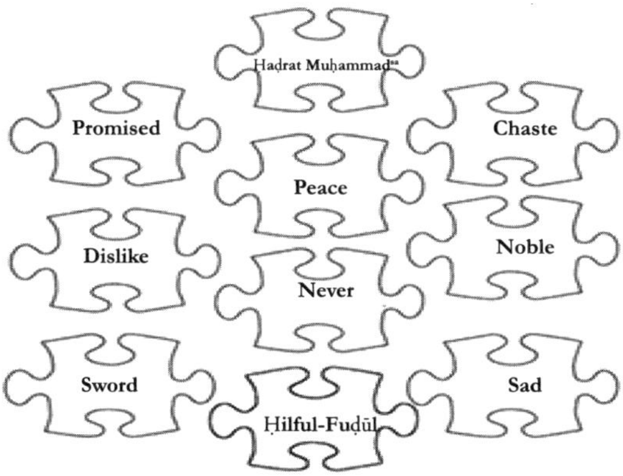

FAMILY TREE

Fill in the blanks with the correct name to help complete the Prophet Muhammad's[sa] family tree.

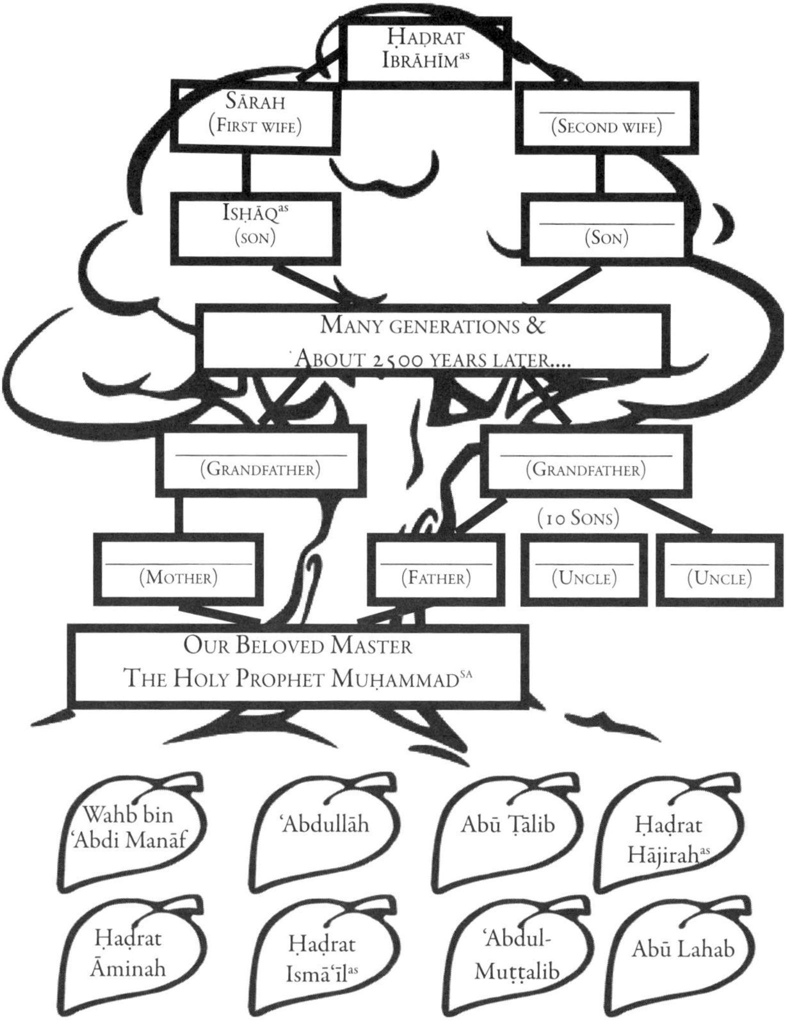

MAKKAH BEFORE THE PROPHET[SA]

Before the coming of the Holy Prophet Muḥammad[sa], Makkah was very different from the way it is now. Choose the number next to the correct statements about what Makkah was like prior to the coming of the Holy Prophet[sa].

1. The Ka'bah was reconstructed by Ḥaḍrat Ibrāhīm[as] and Ḥaḍrat Ismā'īl[as]
2. Everyone in Makkah worshipped only Allah.
3. Hubul, the king of the idols, was placed on the roof of the Ka'bah.
4. The Adhān was given before prayers.
5. People would do Ṭawāf around the Ka'bah naked!
6. People used to have their own idols in their homes, which were basically shapeless stones.

MAZE

Help the caravan find it's way to Makkah!

STUDY QUESTIONS 

1.) Who was Ibrāhīm[as] and what was his relationship with Ismā'īl[as]?

____

____.

2.) What was the famous prayer of Ḥaḍrat Ibrāhīm[as] which was fulfilled in the form of the advent of the Holy Prophet[sa]? _______

____

____.

3.) Who was Ḥaḍrat Hājirah[as]? ___________________________

____.

4.) Why did Ḥaḍrat Ibrāhīm[as] leave Ḥaḍrat Hājirah[as] and her son in the desert? ____

____

____.

5.) How did they survive in the desert? ____________________

____

____

6.) What was the famous water spring, which laid the foundation of the city of Makkah?_______________________.

9.) Where is the Holy Ka'bah located? _____________________

____.

10.) At the birth of the Holy Prophet[sa], his grandfather took him to the Ka'bah and announced that his name is Muḥammad. How did the people of Quraish respond? ______________________

____

____.

11.) What is a wet nurse? Why did the people of Quraish send their children away to the mountains? ____________________

____

____

____.

12.) Who was Ḥalīmah? ____________________________________.

13.) Describe how he Holy Prophet[sa] was different from other children. Give a few examples.____________________________

____

____

____

____.

14.) What was ***Ḥilful -Fuḍūl***, and why was it created and by whom? ____

____

____.

15.) Why didn't this organization succeed? __________________

____

____.

16.) What was the name of the only member who fulfilled this pledge until the end of his life? ______________________.

17.) What do the Arabic words 'Ṣādiq' and 'Amīn' mean?

____

____.

18.) These titles were used for a special person. Do you know his name? ______________________________________.

19.) Who was Ḥaḍrat Khadījah[ra]? ______________________

____.

20.) Why was she called 'Ṭāhirah'?______________________

____

____.

21.) How did Ḥaḍrat Khadījah[ra] get to know of the Holy Prophet Muḥammad[sa]? _____________________________________

____.

22.) Briefly describe how she married the Holy Prophet Muḥammad[sa]. _____________________________________

____.

23.) The Holy Prophet[sa] was known for his mediation skills. Describe an incident where his wisdom prevented the Makkans from a war over the rebuilding of the Ka'bah. ______________________

____

____.

24.) Who was Zaid[ra]? ____

____.

25.) What was his relationship with the Holy Prophet Muḥammad[sa]?

____

____

____.

26.) Why did Ḥaḍrat Zaid[ra] not go back to his parents? _________

____

____

____.

27.) The Holy Ka'bah was built for the worship of ONE God, but at the time of the Holy Prophet's[sa] advent, it was being used for a very different purpose. Do you know what it was? ____________

____

____.

28.) How many idols were present inside the Holy Ka'bah?______.

29.) Who was 'Hubul'? How did it get to Makkah? ____________

____

____.

30.) How did the Arabs treat their idols? Provide a few examples.

____

____

____

____.

31.) The Arabs indulged in many bad habits and customs. Provide a few examples. ____
____
____.

32.) Where would the Holy Prophet[sa] go to meditate?
____.

33.) What was the name of the angel that visited the Holy Prophet[sa] in the cave? ____.

34.) The angel asked him to recite a few words. Do you remember them? ____
____
____.

35.) How did Ḥaḍrat Khadījah[ra] react when the Holy Prophet[sa] told her about what had happened in the cave? ______________
____
____
____.

36.) Who was Waraqah bin Naufal? _________________________
____
____.

37.) What did he predict about the Holy Prophet[sa]? ___________
____
____
____.

38.) In this book, you have learnt about many important people and their qualities. Can you find three qualities that appeal to you and explain why and how you can implement them into your life?